The Government of China

Yu Bin

Mason Crest
Philadelphia

CHINa
THE EMERGING SUPERPOWER

The Government of China

Yu Bin

Mason Crest
Philadelphia

Mason Crest
370 Reed Road
Broomall, PA 19008
www.masoncrest.com

Copyright © 2013 by Mason Crest, an imprint of National Highlights, Inc.
All rights reserved.
Printed and bound in the United States of America.

CPSIA Compliance Information: Batch #CH2013-8.
For further information, contact Mason Crest at 1-866-MCP-Book.

First printing

1 3 5 7 9 8 6 4 2

Library of Congress Cataloging-in-Publication Data

  Yu, Bin.
   The government of China / Yu Bin.
    p. cm. — (China: the emerging superpower)
   Includes bibliographical references and index.
   ISBN 978-1-4222-2161-7 (hardcover)
   ISBN 978-1-4222-2172-3 (pbk.)
   ISBN 978-1-4222-9450-5 (ebook)
   1. China—Politics and government—1976—-Juvenile literature. I. Title. II. Series.

DS779.26.Y73 2012
320.951—dc22

                                  2010047752

Table of Contents

Introduction

Dr. Jianwei Wang
University of Wisconsin–Stevens Point

Before his first official visit to the United States in December 2003, Chinese premier Wen Jiabao granted a lengthy interview to the *Washington Post*. In that interview, he observed: "If I can speak very honestly and in a straightforward manner, I would say the understanding of China by some Americans is not as good as the Chinese people's understanding of the United States." Needless to say, Mr. Wen was making a sweeping generalization. From my personal experience and observation, some Americans understand China at least as well as some Chinese understand the United States. But overall there remains some truth in Mr. Wen's remarks. For example, if you visited a typical high school in China, you would probably find that students there know more about the United States than their American counterparts know about China. For one thing, most Chinese teenagers start learning English in high school, while only a very small fraction of American high school students will learn Chinese.

In a sense, the knowledge gap between Americans and Chinese about each other is understandable. For the Chinese, the United States is the most important foreign country, representing not just the most developed economy, unrivaled military might, and the most advanced science and technology, but also a very attractive political and value system, which many Chinese admire. But for Americans, China is merely one of many foreign countries. As citizens of the world's sole superpower, Americans naturally feel less compelled to learn from others. The Communist nature of the Chinese polity also gives many Americans pause. This gap of interest in and motivation to learn about the other side could be easily detected by the mere fact that every year tens of thousands of Chinese young men and women apply for a visa to study in the United States. Many of them decide to stay in this country. In comparison, many fewer Americans want to study in China, let alone live in that remote land.

Nevertheless, for better or worse, China is becoming more and more important to the United States, not just politically and economically, but also culturally. Most notably, the size of the Chinese population in the United States has increased steadily. China-made goods as well as Chinese food have become a part of most Americans' daily life. China is now the second-largest trade partner of the United States and will be a huge market for American goods and services. China is also one of the largest creditors, with about $1 trillion in U.S. government securities. Internationally China could either help or hinder American foreign policy in the United Nations, on issues ranging from North Korea to non-proliferation of weapons of mass destruction. In the last century, misperception of this vast country cost the United States dearly in the Korean War and the Vietnam War. On the issue of Taiwan, China and the United States may once again embark on a collision course if both sides are not careful in handling the dispute. Simply put, the state of U.S.-China relations may well shape the future not just for Americans and Chinese, but for the world at large as well.

The purpose of this series, therefore, is to help high school students form an accurate, comprehensive, and balanced understanding of China, past and present, good and bad, success and failure, potential and limit, and culture and state. At least three major images will emerge from various volumes in this series.

First is the image of traditional China. China has the longest continuous civilization in the world. Thousands of years of history produced a rich and sophisticated cultural heritage that still influences today's China. While this ancient civilization is admired and appreciated by many Chinese as well as foreigners, it can also be heavy baggage that makes progress in China difficult and often very costly. This could partially explain why China, once the most advanced country in the world, fell behind during modern times. Foreign encroachment and domestic trouble often plunged this ancient nation into turmoil and war. National rejuvenation and restoration of the historical greatness is still considered the most important mission for the Chinese people today.

Second is the image of Mao's China. The establishment of the People's Republic of China in 1949 marked a new era in this war-torn land. Initially the Communist regime was quite popular and achieved significant accomplishments by bringing order and stability back to Chinese society. When Mao declared that the "Chinese people stood up" at Tiananmen Square, "the sick man of East Asia" indeed reemerged on the world stage as a united and independent power. Unfortunately, Mao soon plunged the country into endless political campaigns that climaxed in the disastrous Cultural Revolution. China slipped further into political suppression, diplomatic isolation, economic backwardness, and cultural stagnation.

Third is the image of China under reform. Mao's era came to an abrupt end after his death in 1976. Guided by Deng Xiaoping's farsighted and courageous policy of reform and openness, China has experienced earth-shaking changes in the last quarter century. With the adoption of a market economy, in just two decades China transformed itself into a global economic powerhouse. China has also become a full-fledged member of the international community, as exemplified by its return to the United Nations and its accession to the World Trade Organization. Although China is far from being democratic as measured by Western standards, overall it is now a more humane place to live, and the Chinese people have begun to enjoy unprecedented freedom in a wide range of social domains.

These three images of China, strikingly different, are closely related with one another. A more sophisticated and balanced perception of China needs to take into consideration all three images and the process of their evolution from one to another, thus acknowledging the great progress China has made while being fully aware that it still has a long way to go. In my daily contact with Americans, I quite often find that their views of China are based on the image of traditional China and of China under Mao—they either discount or are unaware of the dramatic changes that have taken place. Hopefully this series will allow its readers to observe the following realities about China.

First, China is not black and white, but rather—like the United States—complex and full of contradictions. For such a vast country, one or two negative stories in the media often do not represent the whole picture. Surely the economic reforms have reduced many old problems, but they have also created many new problems. Not all of these problems, however, necessarily prove the guilt of the Communist system. Rather, they may be the result of the very reforms the government has been implementing and of the painful transition from one system to another. Those who would view China through a single lens will never fully grasp the complexity of that country.

Second, China is not static. Changes are taking place in China every day. Anyone who lived through Mao's period can attest to how big the changes have been. Every time I return to China, I discover something new. Some things have changed for the better, others for the worse. The point I want to make is that today's China is a very dynamic society. But the development in China has its own pace and logic. The momentum of changes comes largely from within rather than from without. Americans can facilitate but not dictate such changes.

Third, China is neither a paradise nor a hell. Economically China is still a developing country with a very low per capita GDP because of its huge population. As the Chinese premier put it, China may take another 100 years to catch up with the United States. China's political system remains authoritarian and can be repressive and arbitrary. Chinese people still do not have as much freedom as American people enjoy, particularly when it comes to expressing opposition to the government. So China is certainly not an ideal society, as its leaders used to believe (or at least declare). Yet the Chinese people as a whole are much better off today than they were 25 years ago, both economically and politically. Chinese authorities were fond of telling the Chinese people that Americans lived in an abyss of misery. Now every Chinese knows that this is nonsense. It is equally ridiculous to think of the Chinese in a similar way.

Finally, China is both different from and similar to the United States. It is true that the two countries differ greatly in terms of political and social systems and cultural tradition. But it is also true that China's program of reform and openness has made these two societies much more similar. China is largely imitating the United States in many aspects. One can easily detect the convergence of the two societies in terms of popular culture, values, and lifestyle by walking on the streets of Chinese cities like Shanghai. With ever-growing economic and other functional interactions, the two countries have also become increasingly interdependent. That said, it is naïve to expect that China will become another United States. Even if China becomes a democracy one day, these two great nations may still not see eye to eye on many issues.

Understanding an ancient civilization and a gigantic country such as China is always a challenge. If this series kindles readers' interest in China and provides them with systematic information and thoughtful perspectives, thus assisting their formation of an informed and realistic image of this fascinating country, I am sure the authors of this series will feel much rewarded.

Tourists walk around the outside of the Imperial Palace, part of the Forbidden City in Beijing. For more than 500 years, emperors of the Ming and Qing dynasties ruled China from this complex of palaces and buildings.

Chinese Traditional Culture and the Dynastic System

China, a vast country that covers some 3.7 million square miles (9.5 million square kilometers) of territory in East Asia, is geographically about the same size as the United States. In recent years these two giant states, located on opposite sides of the Northern Hemisphere, have become increasingly connected. By 2010, for example, the United States was China's largest trade partner, receiving nearly 20 percent of Chinese exports. China, meanwhile, was the second-largest trade partner of the United States, behind only Canada. Diplomatic relations between the two countries—which were nonexistent during several tense decades in the middle of the 20th century—have recently assumed major importance as well.

China is a key player in efforts to defuse tensions on the Korean Peninsula, a regional issue in which the United States has an important interest. China also pledged $150 million in aid for the rebuilding of Afghanistan following the 2001 U.S. invasion that ousted that country's radical Islamist regime and the al-Qaeda terrorists it harbored.

Such ties notwithstanding, China and the United States are profoundly different in crucial respects. As a country, America is young, dynamic, and forward looking, while China is an ancient civilization that remains deeply enmeshed in its past, constantly looking to history for wisdom and guidance. Americans tend to be individually oriented and value personal freedom and liberty above all; in Chinese culture the individual has long taken a backseat to family and social harmony. And, most significant for the purposes of this book, China has a dramatically different political system and form of government from that of the United States or other Western nations.

Understanding China has always proved a daunting challenge for people in the West, even specialists. But this much is certain: one cannot hope to form an accurate picture of modern China in the absence of some background about China's traditional culture.

Characteristics of Chinese Traditional Culture

China is by no means a mere nation-state, but a "cultural universe" of its own category in many respects. China's traditional dynastic system emerged in the third century B.C. and endured until 1911. In the West, by contrast, a succession of territorial entities arose, each becoming a focal point of Western civilization and culture for a time before receding into relative obscurity as another entity ascended to a position of primacy. The longevity of China's traditional system is unparalleled: in the words of Kenneth

Lieberthal, a leading China specialist at the University of Michigan, it would be "as if, in Western terms, the Roman empire had evolved but nevertheless survived into the twentieth century."

The philosophical underpinnings of China's traditional system predate by several centuries the actual unification of China in 221 B.C. No single thinker had a more profound influence on the shape of traditional China than Confucius (Kong Zi), a teacher and philosopher from the small state of Lu. Confucius (551–479 B.C.) lived near the end of the Spring and Autumn period, a time in Chinese history when central authority was weak and various autonomous states around the Yellow River valley fought one another for supremacy. This period of instability and continual warfare led scholars such as Confucius to emphasize the need for order, harmony, and appropriate conduct by rulers and ruled alike. Although his ideas would later form the foundation of traditional Chinese culture and governance, Confucius was—like many great thinkers—largely ignored by his contemporaries. Not until the Han dynasty (206 B.C.–A.D. 220) was Confucianism adopted and developed into an all-encompassing state ideology.

This portrait depicts Confucius, whose philosophy shaped Chinese ideas about government and society for more than 2,000 years.

The role of Confucianism in shaping traditional governance and culture in China can be seen in a number of areas. To begin, Confucianism is remarkably secular. Confucius himself resisted speculation about the nature of the afterlife, and Confucianism explicitly states that morally correct or incorrect behavior should be rewarded or punished in this life. As a result, traditional Chinese politics based on Confucianism was secular from the start. By contrast, religion—specifically Christianity—was inextricably linked to governance and politics in the West until the end of the Middle Ages (roughly the 15th century); and Islamic society has never fully separated religious and state authority.

In the absence of religious elements, what was the carrier of moral codes in traditional China? The answer is education. Confucius and his followers believed that humans are by nature neither good nor bad, but rather shaped by their experience. Education, according to Confucianism, is the key to instilling morality and ensuring appropriate behavior.

In the political realm, education also had a major role to play, in the view of Confucianists. Good governance, according to Confucianism, begins with the virtuous example of rulers, and virtue is cultivated through education. In addition, while ultimate authority in China's traditional dynastic system lay with the emperor—which of course was a hereditary position—thousands of bureaucrats were needed to actually administer the realm, and these men were selected based on their educational qualifications. As China's dynastic system evolved, a four-level examination system based largely on knowledge of the Confucian classics was instituted to select qualified government bureaucrats; it was open to all Chinese men, regardless of their station in life. Those who passed the exam at the lowest level were eligible for official appointment or could proceed to the next level; those who successfully completed all four levels might land a top position at the imperial court.

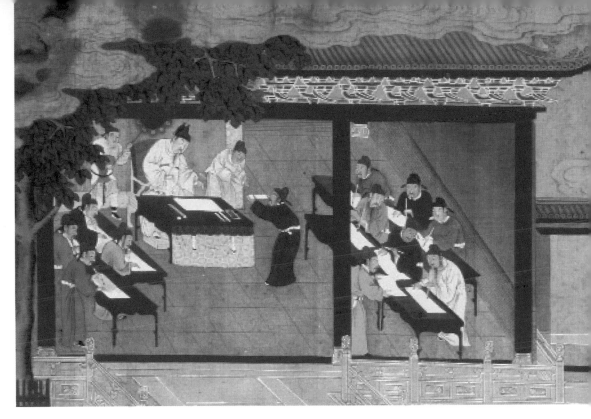

Four-level civil service examinations, which were based largely on knowledge of the Confucian classics, underpinned traditional China's merit-based bureaucracy. This painting on silk depicts a civil-service exam during the Song dynasty (960–1279).

In actuality, however, most of those who passed the official exams at various levels would never get an official position. Instead, they usually resided in their home village or town as part of the "gentry" class—enjoying not only the respect of their neighbors but also exemptions from taxation and compulsory service on state projects. The crucial function of the gentry was that it constituted an unofficial part of the political system, mediating between a thinly structured official bureaucracy (about 20,000 appointed bureaucrats throughout China) and the vast society in traditional China. The gentry were supposed to provide an ethical and virtuous model for the locals, to mediate their disputes, and to help the county magistrate—the lowest level of public official—in managing local affairs. By no means was China's traditional politics democratic. It was, nonetheless, a system based on merit rather than heredity.

Another key element of Confucianism is the emphasis on hierarchical relationships. In the political and social spheres, including within the family, superior-subordinate relationships were clearly defined and dictated proper interactions. For example, sons were subordinate to fathers, and females were subordinate to males; older people were superior to younger people, officials to the masses, and the emperor to everyone else. (An interesting linguistic manifestation of the hierarchical nature of traditional Chinese society can be found in the practice of always using a modifier such as "elder" or "younger" when addressing a brother or sister.) Superiors were due respect and obedience. Everyone was expected to know and observe the proper forms in social interactions, and education was the key to instilling the concept of hierarchy in the minds of the Chinese people. "Equality" was not part of the Confucian vocabulary. Reciprocity, however, was an indispensable part of Chinese life. For while superiors (emperor, official, gentry, father, elder) expected obedience and respect from subordinates (masses, children, younger generation, and so on), they in turn were expected to provide a moral and behavioral example of virtue, modesty, assistance, and protection.

Confucianism was not the only moral code and political philosophy in traditional China. Buddhism, Daoism, Legalism, and later Christianity and Islam all emerged in or came to China. None, however, came close to matching Confucianism's dominant role.

Traditional Political Structure

China was first unified in 221 B.C. by Qin Shi Huang Di (the Qin Emperor). By any standard, the first emperor was a remarkable ruler. He conquered other states; developed a centralized bureaucracy; constructed roads, canals, and the Great Wall of China, which linked the defensive walls built separately by some northern and northwestern states; established a standard written script and a single currency; and standardized weights and measures.

Qin was the only Chinese dynasty that did not utilize Confucianism as its governing ideology. Instead, the philosophical foundation of the Qin dynasty was a school of thought known as Legalism (*fa jia*). The Legalists believed that humans are by nature evil and selfish and will behave badly unless they fear punishment or desire a reward. Whereas the ideal Confucian ruler demonstrated benevolence and virtue and led by his moral example, Legalism denied any harmony of interests between rulers and ruled. Only by consistently enforcing clear laws—particularly through harsh and cruel punishment of transgressors—could society be kept in order, the Legalists maintained.

In keeping with the Legalist philosophy, Qin rule was harsh and authoritarian, and a huge, costly army had to be maintained. In addition, Qin Shi Huang Di's many construction projects—including roads and canals, the Great Wall, and an enormous tomb complex for the emperor—required endless taxation and compulsory service from the peasants. Conditions on the Great Wall were especially brutal: it is estimated that as many as 100,000 conscripted workers lost their lives during the course of the massive construction project. Resentment of Qin rule was widespread, and the state's resources were stretched beyond the limit. The Qin turned out to be the shortest-lived dynasty in China's history: after a scant 14 years, it was overthrown in a popular uprising.

The emperor Qin Shi Huang Di unified China in 221 B.C. The short-lived Qin dynasty (221–207 B.C.) was the only Chinese dynasty that did not use Confucianism as its governing ideology (it was instead guided by the philosophy of Legalism). Nonetheless, the Qin dynasty's legacy was significant.

Despite its brief tenure, the Qin had a lasting impact on later Chinese dynasties; almost all post-Qin rulers, for example, maintained extensive bureaucracies. But the principal mode of governance was switched from Legalism-based coercion to Confucianism-based rule by virtue and moral example. (Of course, laws remained as part of the governing mechanism for deterrence and punishment, but they were not the primary focus.) From the Han dynasty (206 B.C.–A.D. 220), which followed the Qin, to China's final dynasty, the Qing (1644–1911), a three-level socio-political structure of imperial court, bureaucracy, and ordinary people (*bai xing*) gradually took shape.

According to Confucius, the emperor was supposed to be a benevolent ruler, taking care of the state and the people. Of course, some emperors proved to be more benevolent—and more capable—than others. From time to time, corruption, mismanagement, neglect, or abuse of power on the part of an emperor led to a rebellion by his subjects, particularly the peasants. Confucian morality, though it emphasized obedience to legitimate authority, permitted rebellion against a bad ruler. According to Confucianism, a ruler's legitimacy to govern stemmed from the "Mandate of Heaven," which would be withdrawn if the ruler did not govern properly. In the event that a rebellion succeeded, that in itself would be proof that the deposed emperor did not have the Mandate of Heaven to rule.

Almost all the dynasties in Chinese history were ultimately overturned by peasant rebellions. But while dynasties came and went, China's traditional political system endured, remaining remarkably stable for two millennia. To a large degree, this can be explained by the order and continuity brought by the bureaucracy. Indeed, with the bureaucracy mediating between the emperor at the top and the common people at the bottom of society, the traditional Chinese system could afford to have a not-so-capable emperor.

By any standard, the Chinese traditional bureaucracy was an extraordinary accomplishment. The government officials, along with the gentry who assisted them in administering imperial China, were educated people instilled with a common sense of political responsibility, a common moral code, and a shared set of communication skills. According to China scholar Kenneth Lieberthal, many of the characteristics of the Chinese imperial bureaucracy are incorporated in modern Western bureaucracies, including "highly defined offices, merit-based appointments, clearly articulated reward structures, considerable specialization in functions, highly developed formal systems of communications, detailed rules concerning proper lines of authority, regularized reporting obligations, formalized structures for monitoring compliance and deviance, and so forth."

Traditional Foreign Relations: The Tributary System

Until the Western powers expanded their influence into East Asia in the 19th century, China managed to maintain a distinctive regional international system, with itself at the center of a cultural (as opposed to a geopolitical) empire. In this hierarchical system, which was based on the practice of Confucianism, neighboring states were supposed to acknowledge China's cultural superiority through a tributary system. Every few years, rulers of these neighboring states would send emissaries to Beijing; the emissaries would bring as tribute expensive local goods while also offering verbal recognition of China's supremacy. As part of the official ritual, the emperor in Beijing would reciprocate by offering gifts to the tributary emissaries; this was meant to be a token of appreciation of the subordinating states' submission to China's moral authority.

Within this China-centered cultural empire, there was no equality between China and the other states. Nevertheless, the hierarchal tributary system functioned with a remarkable degree of aloofness on the part of China. China was not interested in managing the internal affairs of its tributary states, and it rarely intervened directly; once the ritual was complete, the tributary states enjoyed considerable autonomy in conducting their own affairs. By contrast, the modern Western inter-state system, starting from the 1648 Treaty of Westphalia, recognized the sovereignty and equality of each nation-state in principle, but in practice was based on the ability of nation-states to wage war on one another; those states with the most military power typically imposed their will on weaker states. In imperial China, on the other hand, principle and practice were arguably more consistent. As with its domestic policy, China's foreign policy was founded on the Confucian values of hierarchy, order, and rule by virtue—although to a certain extent military power also underpinned China's position, as tributary states became tributary states through conquest or the threat of conquest.

The culture-based tributary system was relatively stable. In large measure this is because China, the strongest power, had comparatively little incentive to expand territorially. China's highly developed agricultural economy was largely self-sufficient and required little exchange with the outside world. In addition, imperial China regarded itself as the center of civilization, the "Middle Kingdom," which was surrounded by "barbarians" who had nothing of essential value to offer. In the West, by contrast, trade considerations—particularly the acquisition of raw materials and markets—spurred large-scale exploration, conquest, and colonization from the 15th century onward.

Interestingly, for a brief period during the Ming dynasty, China was well ahead of any European nation as a maritime power. Between 1405 and 1433, Admiral Zheng He (1372–1433) conducted seven large voyages of trade and exploration to lands in the Indian Ocean, the Arabian Peninsula, and East Africa. In every respect, Zheng's expeditions dwarfed those of the Spanish and Portuguese mariners whose later voyages would spark what Westerners call the Age of Discovery: Zheng's largest vessels exceeded 400 feet in length, probably five times the length of Columbus's first flagship, the *Santa Maria*; Zheng's fleet consisted of up to 300 vessels (Columbus had 3 ships in 1492); and Zheng's crew totaled between 20,000 and 30,000 (Columbus commanded some 90 sailors on his first voyage). Through its command of the seas, China could well have become the world's foremost commercial and colonial power. But after Zheng's death, the Ming emperor burned his entire fleet and prohibited all further oceangoing voyages, upon pain of death. The Middle Kingdom's traditional sense of aloofness and cultural superiority had prevailed over the inclination to engage with the world.

Challenge from the West

China may have believed that the "barbarians" outside its borders had nothing of value to offer the Middle Kingdom, but while imperial China maintained its traditional ways in self-imposed isolation, the West was advancing steadily in industry, technology, and capitalist development—which generated both momentum for expansion into non-Western parts of the world and the means to carry out that expansion.

China's contacts with the West date back to the Han dynasty, when the Silk Road—the set of overland trade routes across Central Asia—was first open. But large-scale Western intrusion into China did not occur until the early 19th century, when European powers sought trade relations that China did not want. In the end, the West imposed its will on the Middle Kingdom, which ultimately spelled the end of China's dynastic system.

To be sure, Western intrusion into China was by no means the only cause for the final collapse of the Chinese traditional system

The Great Wall, China's most famous landmark, was built to protect the western and northern frontier from invasion by "barbarians." Imperial China considered itself the center of civilization and believed that the cultures outside its borders had nothing of essential value to offer. While Chinese emperors exacted tribute from their weaker neighbors in areas such as present-day Korea and Vietnam, they showed no interest in managing the internal affairs of these states.

and China-centered regional system. Large-scale peasant rebellions, particularly the Bai Lian (White Lotus) Rebellion (1796–1804) and the Taiping Rebellion (1850–1864), drained the resources of the Qing court. The latter almost captured Beijing. Nevertheless, if events proceeded through the usual cycle of dynastic change, the Qing would be replaced by the victors of the social upheaval and peasant rebellion, and the Confucianist system would continue.

However, the coming of the West completely changed the rules of the game that China had played for thousands of years, both with itself and with other states. The West challenged China in three major ways: culturally, economically, and militarily. In the first place, the West rejected China's assertion of cultural and moral superiority over other nation-states and advocated the principle of equality. From the beginning, the Europeans, particularly the British and French, refused to kowtow to the emperor. Nor were they willing to follow the tributary system, which placed all other nations in a subordinate position within the China-centered cultural universe. Thus, the West, for the first time in China's history, imposed an entirely different mechanism of interaction with the Middle Kingdom.

Secondly, the West broke China's economic self-sufficiency by first demanding and then imposing its own "free trade" practices. By the early 19th century, Britain, then the dominant power of the world, ran a huge trade deficit because of its growing taste for China's tea, silk, and porcelain. China, however, wanted almost nothing from the British. In order to offset the trade imbalance, the British resorted to smuggling opium—which was produced in British-colonized India—into China. By the 1830s opium consumption in coastal China had reached such proportions that China, not Britain, was suffering from a trade deficit.

Finally, the West reduced China to a semi-colonial state by crushing the Qing in a series of military conflicts and then imposing disadvantageous treaty terms upon the defeated Chinese. The first of these conflicts, the Opium War, began in 1839 after the Qing government, alarmed at the growing numbers of Chinese opium addicts, banned the smuggling of the narcotic drug. The British Parliament seized the opportunity to declare war on China, and the smaller but better-equipped British military soundly defeated the Chinese. Britain extracted commercial concessions, territory (Hong Kong), and financial rewards (indemnities) from the vanquished Chinese in the 1842 Treaty of Nanjing, which set the pattern for a succession of so-called unequal treaties that China would sign with foreign powers (including France, the United States, Russia, and

This engraving, originally published in a September 1860 issue of *Illustrated London News*, shows British and Russian forces fighting the Chinese army near Beijing during the Second Opium War. Throughout the 19th century, Europeans handed the Chinese a series of humiliating military defeats, in the process taking away territory and forcing China's Qing emperors to sign disadvantageous treaties.

Germany, in addition to Great Britain) in the coming decades. In many of these treaties, China made what in retrospect would turn out to be major economic and territorial concessions in order to preserve its traditional cultural order.

In the aftermath of the Opium War and other defeats, the Qing government did try to introduce some Western learning and technology into China through the so-called Self-Strengthening Movement (1860s to 1890s). This was done, however, only in a halfhearted way. It never occurred to the gentry and bureaucracy that China's rigid and conservative Confucianist system might itself be the problem. Qing officials continued to treat Western learning and practice as *Yong* (for "use" or practical purposes), while keeping Chinese learning as *Ti* (meaning "essence"). When the Qing court finally turned to more radical reforms in the early 20th century by abolishing the Confucianist exam system, it was too little and too late for the politically corrupt, financially broken, and morally bankrupt traditional system.

Troops from the United States, Japan, Italy, Great Britain, and other nations assemble outside the Forbidden City in Beijing to celebrate their victory over the Chinese rebels known as the Boxers, November 1900. The treaty that ended the Boxer Rebellion forced the Chinese government to compensate the Western powers financially and permit them to station troops within China.

The Search for Modernization

By the last decade of the 19th century, China had suffered a series of setbacks as a result of its encounters with foreign countries, beginning with the Opium War. Significant pieces of China's territory had been lost (Great Britain, for example, had taken Hong Kong and part of the Kowloon Peninsula). In addition, China had been forced to open ports to foreign trade, and trade conditions were dictated by the foreigners. China had also been forced to allow foreign diplomatic representatives in Beijing, and foreign citizens living in China were exempt from Chinese law (which is called extraterritoriality). But China would suffer more setbacks before the moribund Qing dynasty finally collapsed.

In 1894 China and Japan went to war over Korea, which for centuries had been a Chinese tributary state. In contrast to China, whose Self-Strengthening

Movement had been largely ineffectual, Japan had pursued a sweeping campaign to modernize following its return to imperial rule in 1868 (the Meiji Restoration). The results were starkly evident on the battlefield, when an industrialized Japan soundly defeated its much larger neighbor, which had basically continued to cling to its traditional ways. Japan imposed harsh and humiliating peace terms on China in the Treaty of Shimonoseki, signed in April 1895. China was forced to cede Taiwan and the Pescadores Islands to Japan, allow Japanese investors to open factories in China, and pay a huge indemnity to Japan.

By 1898, foreign powers had further encroached on Chinese sovereignty. Russia obtained leases for Lüshun (Port Arthur) and Dalian,

This illustration depicts Japanese troops attacking the Chinese garrison at Penyang during the Sino-Japanese War of 1894–1895.

ports on the Liaodong Peninsula; Germany received a concession on the Shandong Peninsula; and Great Britain added the New Territories, several hundred islands and area on the Chinese mainland north of Hong Kong.

At the turn of the 20th century, anti-foreigner violence broke out in China, leading to the conflict that in the West would be known as the Boxer Rebellion. Originally an anti-Qing secret society, the Boxers—or "Yi He Quan" (the Righteous and Harmonious Fists) in Chinese—killed Christian missionaries and other foreigners and, with support from the Qing government, began besieging Western legations by the late spring of 1900. Austria, Italy, France, Germany, Great Britain, Russia, Japan, and the United States responded by sending troops—the total number would ultimately exceed 40,000—to relieve the legations and suppress the uprising. After a few months of fighting, the international coalition had defeated the Boxers and occupied Beijing. The Boxer Protocol, the peace agreement that officially ended the conflict, was yet another humiliating treaty China had to sign; among other conditions, it forced China to accept foreign troops on its soil and imposed a huge indemnity.

Republicanism and Chaos

After experiencing decades of military defeats, loss of territory, and blows to its sense of national pride, China was ripe for change. A small but quickly growing nationalist movement began to emerge across China. For the first time, many believed that it was the territorial and political, not just the cultural, China that had to be saved from further erosion at the hands of foreign powers. And for many Chinese nationalists, particularly the educated, the Qing dynasty embodied more than just the outdated Confucianist culture. The dynasty—established by Manchus who swept down from the northeast and conquered China in the 17th century—itself represented foreign rule on China's land. It, too, had to be overthrown.

China's most prominent nationalist was Sun Yat-sen, a physician who had received part of his education in Hawaii. In 1894 Sun organized a secret revolutionary society among overseas Chinese. After leading an abortive revolt against the Qing in 1895, he spent the next 16 years abroad, organizing opposition, raising money, and planning for the overthrow of the Manchus. In 1905 Sun and several hundred supporters set up the Tong Meng Hui (Revolutionary League) in Japan. Several unsuccessful attempts were made to topple the Manchus before an uprising in the city of Wuchang on October 10, 1911, unleashed a nationwide anti-Manchu tide that swept the Qing dynasty—and China's 2,000-year-old traditional dynastic system—into the history books.

In place of imperial rule, a republic was established, and Sun was named its provisional president. However, lacking an army, Sun soon realized that he and his revolutionary associates could not maintain order throughout China. In March 1912 Sun resigned as provisional president, making way for Yuan Shikai, a military commander, to assume the presidency. At first, Yuan appeared to support Sun's vision for a republican form of government, but he soon began assuming greater and greater powers for

The Chinese nationalist leader Sun Yat-sen (1866–1925) helped to inspire the movement to overthrow the Qing dynasty and establish a republican government in China.

himself. After parliamentary elections held in 1913 were won by the Guomindang (GMD), or Nationalist Party—a political party that had been established by Sun Yat-sen and his supporters—Yuan ordered the assassination of a top GMD leader and dissolved the parliament. Later he set up a puppet National Assembly that ultimately pronounced him emperor. Although widespread resistance, including opposition from his own military commanders, forced him to step down in March 1916, China had already begun to descend into chaos. Various regional warlords (some with the support of foreign powers hoping to advance their position in China) fought to control the entire country.

China's tragic experience led many young Chinese intellectuals to fundamentally question the utility of Confucianism in the modern world. A majority believed that the only way to attain national salvation was through total Westernization; China, they believed, must learn from "Mr. Science" and "Mr. Democracy," meaning Western technology and the Western political system of representative democracy. Many of these young Chinese intellectuals went to study in Japan, the most Westernized Asian nation. Others went to Western Europe or North America. But many pro-West Chinese turned away from Western liberalism and embraced Marxism, and arguably the most important catalyst for this change was World War I.

Embracing Communism

World War I, which erupted in August 1914, was a savage four-year struggle that claimed millions of lives and challenged Europeans' optimistic outlook regarding the progress of their civilizations. While most of the carnage took place on European battlefields, the war also played out in far-flung regions, including East Asia. Japan, joining the side of the Allies (France, Great Britain, Russia, and other nations fighting Germany, Austria-Hungary, and the Ottoman Empire), seized German holdings in China's Shandong Province in the early months of the war. In early 1915, Japan also presented China with the notorious "Twenty-one Demands," insisting on a whole range of "special privileges" in managing China's internal affairs. Japan's demands fell into five general categories: 1) that China confirm and legitimize Japan's gains in Shandong; 2) that Japan's control of Manchuria be expanded and legalized; 3) that Japan be given exclusive rights to control China's mining facilities and mineral deposits in central China; 4) that no other powers be allowed to acquire or lease any harbor, bay, or island along China's coast; and 5) that Japan be consulted in China's political, military, and economic affairs. Japan's demands, which would transform China into a virtual Japanese colony, angered many Chinese. Yet under the threat of war with their more powerful neighbor, Chinese leaders reluctantly agreed to the Japanese demands in April 1915.

The year 1917 would prove highly significant for China's future. In neighboring Russia, the monarchical regime of the czar—highly unpopular for, among other reasons, its mismanagement of the war—was overthrown, ultimately to be replaced with a Communist system. In August 1917, China joined the Allies, declaring war on Germany and Austria-Hungary and ultimately contributing 100,000 laborers to assist the Allied forces in Europe.

Thus, when Chinese delegates traveled to the Paris Peace Conference in 1919, they took their place with the victorious Allies. The Chinese had good reason to believe that the peace treaty that would ultimately be crafted would restore China's sovereignty over Shandong Province. After all, the Allied nations had conditionally accepted the Fourteen Points—a set of principles for establishing peace, enunciated by U.S. president Woodrow Wilson—which included the ideals of open diplomacy and national self-determination. In the end, however, the European democracies had other ideas. To their dismay, the Chinese delegates discovered that the European allies had made a secret deal with Japan. Article 156 of the Treaty of Versailles—the peace treaty officially ending World War I—specified that the German concession in Shandong Province would be transferred to Japan rather than being returned to China. Between two Asian allies, the Western democracies (with the United States withholding its assent) chose the strong at the expense of the weak, disregarding the principle of national self-determination.

As a result of the events at Versailles, Western liberalism lost its appeal to many young Chinese intellectuals. On May 4, 1919, hundreds of thousands of Chinese college students demonstrated throughout China against the Versailles settlement, spawning a massive upsurge in Chinese nationalism that came to be known as the May Fourth Movement.

It was at this point that Chen Duxiu, dean of Beijing University and founder of the pro-West "New Cultural Movement"—together with many others of his generation—turned to communism. The idea of communism had been pioneered by the German political philosopher Karl Marx (1818–1883), who held that the socio-political reality is determined by material (or economic) conditions rather than by abstract ideals. Marx also argued that private property and market capitalism inevitably result in the absolute poverty of the proletariat (working class), cyclical economic recessions, and heightened "class struggles" between the proletariat (who must sell their labor) and the capitalists (who control the means of production). In Marx's view, communism, a system characterized by the equal distribution of economic goods and the ultimate "withering away" of the state, would inevitably replace capitalism.

Chinese intellectuals were introduced to the ideas and theories of communism principally through the Soviet Union, which was created in the wake of the 1917 Bolshevik Revolution. For many

Chinese who were embittered and disillusioned by recent events, the Soviet model seemed to provide an attractive alternative to Western democratic capitalism. At the same time, however, few in China really understood the essence of Marxism and its Russian variant. They nonetheless embraced it, perhaps because they hated Western imperialism. In 1921 the Chinese Communist Party (CCP) was founded with Chen Duxiu as its first general secretary.

The CCP's Fate and the Russian Factor

In the beginning, the CCP's influence was minimal. Even the Russian Bolsheviks were skeptical about the potential of the Party in what they saw as a backward nation. Marx had said, and the Soviets believed, that a Communist revolution could begin only among the urban proletariat, and only in a country with a mature capitalist system—which made prospects in China (a largely agrarian and only spottily industrialized society) dim. The Soviet Communist leader Joseph Stalin suggested an alliance between the CCP and the much stronger Guomindang, which was led by Sun Yat-sen. By 1923 Sun had come to accept financial and military assistance from the Soviets. He also heeded their advice to ally with the Chinese Communists in order to unify China by defeating the warlords who had emerged after the collapse of the Qing dynasty.

After Sun's death in 1925, he was succeeded as head of the Guomindang by Jiang Jieshi (Chiang Kai-shek), who had earlier studied the Soviet military system in Moscow. In July of 1926, Jiang, commanding the National Revolutionary Army, which was composed of GMD and CCP troops, embarked on a military campaign against the warlords. Within nine months Jiang's army had won control of all of southern China, and in March 1927 Jiang set up a Nationalist government in Nanjing. But in April, after his troops had reached Shanghai, Jiang turned against his erstwhile Communist allies, ordering the

Two major leaders of Russian communism, Vladimir Lenin (left) and Joseph Stalin, meet in 1922, the year the Union of Soviet Socialist Republics (USSR) was formed. The success of the Bolsheviks in establishing a government based on Communist principles attracted many Chinese to the Communist Party during the early 1920s.

massacre of tens of thousands of CCP members (in all, up to 90 percent of China's Communists may have been killed). Clinging to the Bolshevik model, surviving CCP members continued to stage urban revolts in some of China's larger cities, where a small proletariat existed, but all of these revolts were ruthlessly suppressed by Jiang's Nationalist government. Clearly communism was not going to come to China exactly as Karl Marx had envisioned.

Other Communists who had escaped the GMD crackdown fled to China's vast countryside, however. It was there that the CCP not only survived but also started to take root and expand during the late 1920s and 1930s.

But even in the countryside, the small Communist Party and its armed forces, led by some "returned students" trained in the Soviet Union, continued to follow directives from Moscow. They rejected guerrilla tactics in favor of "regular warfare," even when confronted by the superior forces of the GMD after 1931. A series of military defeats eventually forced the CCP to abandon its rural bases in the south and undertake the heroic and tragic retreat dubbed the Long March. Between October of 1934 and October of 1935, the Communist Red Army trekked more than 12,500 kilometers (7,767 miles), much of it over rugged terrain and in harsh conditions. By the time the Red Army reached remote Yan'an in Shaanxi Province, only about 10,000 of the 120,000 who had begun the journey a year earlier were still alive.

During the Long March, however, the CCP replaced its Soviet-trained leaders with homegrown revolutionaries such as Mao Zedong. Mao, a towering figure in 20th-century history, would ultimately guide the CCP to victory in China.

Generalissimo Jiang Jieshi (at right) and his officers examine a map while planning a campaign against the Communists during the 1930s. Many Chinese were outraged at Jiang for seeking to eradicate the Communists instead of fighting Japanese invaders.

The Anti-Japanese War: An Opportunity for the CCP

During the early 1930s, while Jiang Jieshi was busy trying to eliminate the Chinese Communists, Japan was steadily encroaching on Chinese territory. The first incursion came in 1931, when Japanese troops overran Manchuria (three provinces in northeastern China); the following year, Japan set up a puppet state there. Soon Japan began sponsoring autonomy movements in other provinces, demonstrating its continuing designs on Chinese territory. Yet all the while, Jiang avoided engaging the Japanese forces, instead using his Nationalist troops to attack the Chinese Communists. By contrast, Mao Zedong and the CCP called for a unified front against the invaders, and for many ordinary people in China, the notion that Chinese should not fight one another when their national survival was at stake made perfect sense.

Eventually Jiang's policy of fighting against the Chinese Communists rather than the Japanese angered even some of his own generals, who arrested him in December 1936. Under pressure, Jiang agreed to a united front in the fight against the Japanese and, at the urging of the Chinese Communists and the Soviets, was released.

In July 1937 Japan began a massive campaign to conquer China. The Japanese succeeded in capturing and occupying much of China's eastern coastal region (the country's most developed parts). But in eight years of fighting—most of which occurred within the context of World War II (1939–1945)—Japanese forces were unable to subjugate China's vast interior. Nevertheless, the suffering Japan inflicted on the Chinese people was staggering. A particularly well-known—and barbaric—incident occurred after Japanese troops took the city of Nanjing, then China's capital, on December 13, 1937. Over the next two and a half months, Japanese soldiers went on a spree of rape and murder. By the time the notorious "Rape of Nanjing" finally ended, as many as 370,000 men, women, and children (almost all of them noncombatants) had been slaughtered, and up to 80,000 women and girls had been raped. All told, according to one Chinese account, Japanese military activities in the years 1931–1945 directly caused 35 million casualties in China and economic losses of $500 billion.

This terrified baby was one of the few survivors of the Japanese bombing of Shanghai's South Station in August 1937. The Communists won support among ordinary Chinese by resisting the Japanese invasion.

During the long years of Japan's occupation, Jiang Jieshi—despite his 1936 pledge to wage a unified war against the Japanese—largely avoided committing his Nationalist troops in major engagements. After evacuating Nanjing ahead of the Japanese advance, Jiang retreated to China's interior, where he established his headquarters in remote Chongqing. There, protected by the rugged terrain, he bided his time. Although the Allies at war with Germany and Japan (including the United States and Great Britain) named him supreme commander in the China theater and sent him military aid, Jiang conserved materiel and troops for what he believed would be an inevitable postwar showdown with the Chinese Communists.

Meanwhile, the Communists chose to engage the Japanese, thereby winning popular support among the Chinese people. Commanding a poorly equipped peasant army, Mao Zedong was able to conduct an effective campaign of guerrilla warfare against the superior Japanese military. By the time Japan surrendered in 1945, the ranks of the Chinese Communist Party had swelled to more than a million; the CCP's armed forces also exceeded 1 million, and they were supplemented by some 2 million militiamen. The CCP controlled a vast area in northeastern and northwestern China, with a population of 100 million. In the eyes of most Chinese, including many intellectuals, the Communists had shown themselves to be the true nationalists, willing and able to fight for national salvation.

At various points during the war against Japan, the small and weak Communist forces had seemed on the verge of being wiped out. The CCP's survivability can be attributed largely to the policies and strategies it adopted during the war against Japan. One such strategy was the "mass line." In brief, the mass line involved a close relationship between the Communist cadres (trained and indoctrinated Party members) and the ordinary people in a cyclical decision-making and implementation process that might be described as "to the people, from the people, and to the people again." Specifically, the process meant that 1) the cadres should go to the people to find out what actual conditions were and what the people needed; 2) the information gathered from the people, not Marxist-Leninist theory, should then form the basis of policy making; and 3) after policies were made, Communist leaders should go back to the people to help implement the policies as well as to discover any deficiencies that might need to be corrected. The mass line did give an appearance of populism. The relationship between the ruler and the ruled, nonetheless, was not reversed, and the Communists remained a leading force for the Chinese people and society.

Other components of Communist strategy were decentralization, streamlining, and self-reliance. All three were, to a great extent, born of necessity during the war against Japan. Decentralization

Mao Zedong, who became chairman of the Chinese Communist Party in 1935, reviews Communist troops, 1944. Lessons learned in the countryside during the wars with Japan and the Chinese Nationalists would later guide Mao in setting policies for the People's Republic of China.

meant that decision-making power should be given to local officials and commanders (a sensible strategy in the face of unreliable wartime communication). The Communist bureaucracy should be minimized in order to maximize efficiency and flexibility (major advantages when fighting a larger, better-equipped foe). And the individual CCP base areas should be self-sufficient (both because outside assistance could not be counted on and because the CCP did not want to overburden—and potentially alienate—the masses of Chinese peasants from which it drew its main support).

Strategies such as mass line, guerrilla warfare, and self-reliance helped the CCP survive, and even flourish, during the war with

Japan. And, after the Japanese surrender, they also helped the CCP triumph in the civil war with Jiang's Nationalists, which broke out in October 1945. Despite being significantly outnumbered and outgunned, the Communists pushed the Nationalist forces from the northeast, across the Yangtze River, and down to Hainan Island in a matter of three and a half years. In 1949 Jiang and his followers fled to Taiwan.

On October 1, 1949, Mao Zedong proclaimed the establishment of the People's Republic of China (PRC). The CCP had won control of the world's most populous nation. Now the task was to set up structures and institutions for governing this vast land.

An enormous poster of Chairman Mao watches over visitors to Tiananmen Square, Beijing. Mao, who announced the establishment of the People's Republic of China on October 1, 1949, dominated Chinese politics and society until his death in 1976.

3

Political Structure and Dynamics

Since its founding in 1949, the People's Republic of China has remained a Communist country, with the CCP maintaining a monopoly of power. In spite of this, governance in the PRC has gone through wide fluctuations, from the initial adoption of Soviet-style centralized-control communism (1949–1957) to Mao's experiment with a "mass line" populist developmental approach (1958–1961), the total rejection of Soviet bureaucratic communism (1966–1976), and market socialism (1979 to the present). In the 1990s and early 2000s, reform-minded Chinese leaders promoted competitive elections at the village level (and, to a lesser extent, the county level). The results were mixed. Certainly no push toward bottom-up democratization ensued, as some observers had predicted. Similarly, a much-touted push to establish the rule of law, which began after Hu Jintao came to power in 2002, has yet to yield dramatic results.

Adopting the Soviet Model

In classic Marxist thinking, the state (or government) is simply a tool of the capitalist class and will be done away with under communism. In a Communist society, citizens—who are supposed to be strictly equal in political, economic, and social status—rotate in serving the public, so in theory no government is required. Nor, according to classic Marxist theory, are private property or economic markets necessary in a Communist system. Marx predicted that communism would develop only in advanced capitalist states with high-level productive capability (that is, in Europe or North America), and once these countries had become Communist, citizens would be given whatever they needed.

The writings of the German philosopher Karl Marx (1818–1883) formed the basis of communism. Yet when Communist governments actually came to power in the Soviet Union and China, many of Marx's assumptions and predictions proved incorrect.

Marx did not live to see the Bolshevik Revolution or the establishment of the Soviet Union. If he had, he would have seen some of his ideas disproved. The world's first Communist state developed not in an advanced capitalist society but in Europe's poorest nation. In addition, while the Bolsheviks did away with the existing Russian government, they replaced it with a centralized dictatorship. The revolution also led to the nationalization of both the urban and rural economies.

In the Soviet system, the central government (through an extensive bureaucracy) controlled virtually every aspect of governance, economic activity, and social/welfare policy for the entire country; provincial and local governments simply carried out the dictates of the central authorities. Although Russia under the czars had also had a top-down government, under the Soviet leader Joseph Stalin centralized power extended to all localities and penetrated into the lowest levels of society. The Soviet economic system featured a series of so-called Five-Year Plans, by which government officials mapped out the development of the national economy in what they considered a "scientific" and orderly way, allocating resources to various enterprises and specifying which goods would be produced and in what quantities. Using this system of centralized economic planning and direction (what is referred to as a command economy), the Soviets were able to achieve rapid industrialization, particularly in the heavy industrial sectors and arms industry.

Another prominent feature of the Soviet system was the domination of the Communist Party. The only political organization with any power, it functioned as part of an overarching control mechanism, particularly in supervising governmental bureaucracies at all levels. Moreover, Communist Party membership was a requirement for virtually all bureaucratic positions.

In many respects, the experience of the CCP before 1949 had little in common with that of the Soviet Communists. Whereas the Bolsheviks had come to power virtually overnight in 1917, fully 28 years would pass between the founding of the CCP and its ultimate triumph. And during that time, Mao and his comrades developed structures and strategies such as "mass line," decentralization, and self-reliance—which were the antithesis of the Soviet top-down bureaucratic model. Yet after ascending to power in 1949, the CCP

oped coastal area was receiving more investment at the expense of the interior and poorer parts of the country. Last but not least, Mao argued that China might have to reduce its investment in the defense industry in order to make more money available for the civilian sector; eventually, he believed, a stronger national economy might provide a stronger economic basis for China's defense. In sum, Mao thought that a more balanced, long-term, and pragmatic approach to economic development might serve China's efforts to modernize better than rigidly following the Soviet model.

Politically, the top-down Soviet system encouraged a centralized bureaucracy whose inflexible and rather conservative nature was a far cry from the Maoist revolutionary spirit developed during the wartime period. Some Communist cadres, once in the cities living a more comfortable life, became more bureaucratic and corrupted. Mao started to have second thoughts about the Soviet model.

By 1958 Mao had decided to abandon the Soviet model in favor of an approach that was more in keeping with the CCP's pre-1949 experience. Through a massive campaign to raise production—dubbed the Great Leap Forward—Mao believed that China could rapidly catch up economically with Great Britain and the United States, which at the time were the world's leading industrial powers. To achieve its lofty goals, the Great Leap Forward would rely not on the technical expertise of central planners but rather on the revolutionary fervor and ingenuity of the people.

In the summer of 1958, Mao toured central China and was greatly impressed by the grassroots initiatives he saw and by the innovative ways peasants and local Party officials managed their lives. The superiority of the "mass line" strategy that the CCP had earlier emphasized appeared to be reconfirmed.

During the preceding years, the government had gradually collectivized agriculture, so that the vast majority of peasant families were now part of large "agricultural producer cooperatives," or

APCs, typically made up of several hundred households. The income of individual farmers on APCs was determined solely by their labor contributions. For the Great Leap Forward, the government decided to create even larger administrative units in rural areas. Called "people's communes," they ranged in size from several thousand to tens of thousands of households, and—like the Communist base areas during the anti-Japanese war and the civil war with the Nationalists—they were intended to be self-sufficient. Each people's commune had agricultural as well as industrial enterprises; each had its own schools and cafeterias, and many had day care centers and nursing homes so that women could be part of the workforce. Each was responsible for providing its own public security and for administering social welfare programs and medical care for its members. The size and available resources of the people's communes enabled them to undertake large-scale

This 1957 poster includes images of a manufacturing plant, a map of industrial facilities, and charts showing economic growth. In 1958 Mao initiated the Great Leap Forward, an ambitious campaign designed to help China quickly catch up with industrial powers such as Great Britain and the United States. In the end, however, the Great Leap Forward failed dismally, contributing greatly to a nationwide famine that killed millions.

During the 1950s the Chinese government organized peasants into collectives and, eventually, large-scale "people's communes" that were supposed to be self-sufficient. Commune members worked together in fields or rural factories, and everyone received the same pay regardless of productivity.

public-works projects, and to Mao and other CCP leaders, they seemed to be ideal engines for economic growth in the countryside.

But unforeseen problems would plague the people's communes—and ultimately contribute to disaster. First, significant amounts of land and labor were taken out of agricultural production in order to set up and run rural factories. Second, because all commune residents received the same pay, there was little personal incentive to work hard, leading to a decrease in productivity. There was, however, a personal incentive for the commune managers—Communist Party cadres who answered to the central government—to put the best possible face on their achievements. In fact, in order to advance their careers, many commune managers grossly exaggerated the crop yields that had been attained. And this false information was fed through a highly unreliable governmental information channel, in which there was widespread reluctance to report problems. In large measure this reluctance stemmed from the so-called Anti-Rightist Campaign of 1957, during which the government punished hundreds of thousands of Chinese intellectuals for criticizing CCP officials—after Mao himself had solicited such criticism.

The expectation of a bumper harvest, fed by false agricultural production figures, led Mao in 1958 to shift more rural labor to steel production, one of the primary goals of the Great Leap Forward. But instead of ordering the construction of large steel factories, Mao promoted the creation of millions of "backyard furnaces," where Chinese from all walks of life melted down whatever metal they could find (including, in many cases, finished goods) to help fulfill the government's unrealistically high steel quota.

What the backyard furnaces turned out, in spite of the great amount of labor expended, was a large quantity of unusable pig iron. Worse, the labor shift led to a shortage of manpower in rural areas, where crops were often left unharvested in the fields. Meanwhile, commune cafeterias were consuming (and wasting) more food. But most devastatingly, the local cadres continued to impose agricultural taxation based on the false crop surpluses reported by commune managers. Peasants on the communes were forced to surrender, as taxes due to the central government, grain that they desperately needed themselves. Bad weather in 1959 and 1960 compounded the problems, and to make matters even worse, Moscow suspended all economic aid to China in 1960. As a result, Mao's Great Leap Forward ended in a nationwide famine of unprecedented scope: it is estimated that between 1959 and 1962, as many as 30 million Chinese (the majority from the countryside) died of starvation and hunger-related causes. Mao's "mass line" approach to jump-start China's economy had been a catastrophic failure.

In the next few years, as Mao's influence temporarily waned, other CCP officials endeavored to resuscitate China's economy and improve conditions in devastated rural areas. The approach of

Mao Zedong (wearing gray suit) speaks with other top Chinese Communist leaders during a 1962 meeting of the Central Committee of the Chinese Communist Party (CCP) in Beijing. Pictured with Mao (from left to right) are Prime Minister Zhou Enlai, economic planner Chen Yun, President Liu Shaoqi, and CCP general secretary Deng Xiaoping. In the early 1960s, Chinese leaders like Liu and Deng advocated a moderate, pragmatic approach to help China recover from the Great Leap Forward—yet Mao would soon launch another radical and disastrous political campaign.

these officials—who included China's president, Liu Shaoqi, as well as the CCP's general secretary, Deng Xiaoping—was less revolutionary and more pragmatic. Mao's mass line approach was out, and central planning and bureaucratic decision-making were back in. While the people's communes remained in rural areas, actual decision-making power was given to much smaller units, such as production teams and even individual families, who were permitted to cultivate private plots and to sell their produce.

By the mid-1960s, after the Chinese economy had significantly recovered, Mao reemerged to warn China that there were "class enemies" within the CCP. Those enemies, he said, were "revising" true Marxism-Leninism. In 1966 Mao openly called for the removal of those who followed the "revisionist line," meaning those who favored more bureaucratic, "capitalist" approaches (or anything different from his "correct" policies). Thus began the so-called Great Proletarian Cultural Revolution, called the Cultural Revolution for short.

Over the next decade, the Cultural Revolution would wreak havoc on Chinese society. Communist Party leaders and government bureaucrats, intellectuals, and virtually anyone in a position of authority was vulnerable to harassment, humiliation, assault, forced "reeducation," and even death. Educators were among the early victims: in the summer and fall of 1966, students inspired by Mao's call to "thoroughly criticize and repudiate the reactionary bourgeois ideas in the sphere of . . . education," turned on their teachers and school administrators, humiliating and beating them. Eventually schools would be closed entirely, producing a "lost generation" who had missed out on a proper education. In late 1966 and early 1967, bureaucrats, including top leaders such as Liu Shaoqi and Deng Xiaoping, were publicly "condemned" in mass rallies and even physically attacked by the so-called Red Guards, young college and high school students claiming to be most loyal to Mao's "revolutionary line." Bureaucrats in many parts of China quickly became the prime targets of mass groups, many of which competed to claim loyalty to Mao while denouncing others as reactionary. In many parts of China, conflicts between different Red Guard factions soon escalated into real fighting with real weapons. By late 1967 and early 1968, the huge Asian nation was in a state of anarchy, without a functioning government, without a unified ruling party, and even without strong law-enforcement agencies to enforce order. All had become targets for the masses to criticize, to humiliate, and to attack. The Cultural Revolution also split Chinese families, as children denounced their parents, and adults, many under relentless pressure, betrayed family members, friends, and, ultimately, themselves; many committed suicide. All told, hundreds of thousands of Chinese lost their lives in the Cultural Revolution; millions of others, including former bureaucrats, educators, scientists, college students, and high school graduates, were "sent down" to the vast countryside for "reeducation" through manual labor or "integration with the masses." Not until after Mao's death in 1976 would the Cultural Revolution finally be halted.

Like the earlier Great Leap Forward, the Cultural Revolution produced disastrous consequences: a demoralized nation, an economy on the verge of collapse, a generation of uneducated youth, a thoroughly discredited ruling party. Out of this turmoil would emerge a

Chinese peasants take a break from their work to study Mao Zedong's "Little Red Book," a staple of the Cultural Revolution (1966–1976). The Cultural Revolution, instigated by Mao and several influential followers to root out "revisionists," "capitalist roaders," "bourgeois reactionaries," and other supposed enemies of the Communist revolution, plunged China into social chaos.

nation and a political elite that were less ideological and more open-minded and pragmatic.

Rebuild and Reform

Both the Great Leap Forward and the Cultural Revolution can be seen as failures in the mass line approach to policy making—or, perhaps, as failures to apply fully the mass line approach. In the case of the Great Leap Forward, Mao did bypass the normal bureaucracy and appeal directly to the ordinary people (and local Party cadres), and he then formulated policies based on what he believed he had learned, not on orthodox Marxist-Leninist theory. But once policies had been formulated, he did not take the crucial third step in the mass line approach: he did not go back to the people to see what effects the policies were having and to make any needed adjustments. In the case of the Cultural Revolution, Mao again appealed directly to the people, but that is basically where the application of the mass line approach stopped. Indeed, after stirring up the revolutionary fervor of the masses, Mao stood by while they destroyed the Party and state bureaucracies (which may have been his intent). In both cases, the power of a single charismatic leader prevailed over the *system* of government and the ruling Communist Party, revealing a major weakness in China's political structure. The leaders who immediately succeeded Mao would have to confront this legacy.

In 1978 Deng Xiaoping emerged as China's paramount leader. From the beginning of his rule until his death in 1997, Deng advocated a more pragmatic approach, which was encapsulated in a favorite saying of his: "It does not matter whether a cat is black or white, so long as it catches mice." In practical terms, Deng's "cat theory" meant that China would adopt whatever worked for China, be it communism, capitalism, some combination of the two, or some other system. This was a significant departure from Mao's insistence on ideological purity. Yet at a more philosophical level, Deng's cat theory harkened back to Mao's thinking four decades earlier, when the CCP had searched for its own strategy of mass line—that is, when practice, rather than orthodox Marxist teaching or the Soviet approach, was supposed to be the sole guide for policy makers. (It might be argued that, after the founding of the People's Republic of China, Mao had essentially substituted his own rather inflexible revolutionary orthodoxy for Marxism-Leninism.)

Deng's public persona and policy-making style stood in stark contrast with that of the charismatic Mao. Deng never attempted to create a Mao-like "cult of personality." Rather, he tended to maneuver behind the scenes while delegating authority to underlings. Seldom did he trust the popular expression from below, as Mao had done; his policy-making approach was essentially top-down and, most of the time, invisible. If elite politics remained murky and lacked procedural and institutional clarity under Deng, his relationship with other top leaders was no longer a matter of life and death, as had been the rule under Mao. During Deng's era, policy differences between political elites were not resolved through political violence and persecution. Those who were removed from office during the 1980s (for example, Hua Guofeng, Hu Yaobang, and Zhao Ziyang) continued to enjoy their private life after their dismissal. In policy debates, Deng seldom imposed his views upon others, but patiently built a coalition, bargained with other policy groups, and compromised.

Owing largely to the changed political thinking and policy styles under Deng, China achieved sustained political stability, something that it had seldom if ever seen in the 20th century. Political stability, in turn, enabled Deng to focus on economic reform, which became the major thrust of his regime. His initial reforms came in the countryside, where the "household responsibility system" allowed peasants to make decisions regarding what to grow on their land and what to do with their surplus produce. Gradually, the state relinquished its tight control over rural areas by abolishing the people's commune system. In urban areas, Deng sought gradually to replace the old state-controlled command economy with a more market-based one. Whereas state-owned enterprises had dominated China's economy under Mao, Deng experimented with different types of ownership—public, collective, and private—believing they could coexist and even compete in an increasingly open and growing market. Meanwhile, Deng gradually opened up China's economy to foreign trade and investment. Eventually these reforms would lead

After Mao's death, Deng Xiaoping (shown here in a 1975 photo) became China's paramount leader. Advocating a more pragmatic, less ideological approach, Deng—who was twice purged during the Cultural Revolution—set in motion the reforms that have transformed China's economy.

to significantly decreased government involvement in the economic and social spheres, along with increased prosperity and expanded personal freedom for Chinese citizens in the areas of employment, business activities, mobility, and travel.

Though he is remembered primarily as an economic reformer, Deng did pursue limited political reforms (generally in the service of his economic program). As early as 1986, Deng realized that changes in China's political structure would be necessary for economic reform to succeed in the long term. One of the central issues, in Deng's view, was to separate the ubiquitous role of the Communist Party from the state administration. This would be followed by decentralizing policy making and restructuring and streamlining the bureaucracies—institutional reforms that, it was hoped, would make officials more responsive to demands from below. Meanwhile, Deng also tried to modify recruiting methods so that bureaucrats were chosen on the basis of their professional competence, rather than on their "political correctness" alone.

Under Deng, experiments in democratic self-governance were even conducted, albeit at the village level. Beginning in the early 1980s, rural villages began electing members of villagers' committees and representative assemblies (a system of "self-governing" that was formally written into China's state constitution in 1982). This system was a radical departure from the village governing system in the people's communes under Mao, when a few cadres and CCP members made all the important decisions. By 1985 a total of 948,628 villagers' committees existed in China.

There were, however, limits to Deng's embrace of democratic reform. The starkest example came in 1989, when Deng ordered units of China's regular army to forcibly disperse pro-democracy demonstrators in Beijing's Tiananmen Square. Late on the night of June 3 and into the early hours of the following morning, heavily armed People's Liberation Army soldiers cleared Tiananmen Square and, it is believed, fired on student protesters and sympathetic Beijing residents in a series of clashes. Hundreds are thought to have been killed.

The crackdown—which in the West came to be known as the Tiananmen massacre—damaged China's relations with major Western nations and led to economic sanctions by the United States. One of the results of the Tiananmen incident seems to be that both the state and society saw the limit of their actions vis-à-vis one another. The lesson was learned, of course, at a very high cost for both sides.

In the aftermath of the Tiananmen crackdown, Deng resigned from his remaining Communist Party posts. This was a significant milestone—the first time a paramount leader of the CCP had willingly stepped down. Indeed, Deng may have been the first major Communist leader anywhere to retire rather than die in office or be removed by his peers.

Jiang Zemin and Beyond

Jiang Zemin became the CCP general secretary, the highest Party post, in 1989 during the Tiananmen crackdown. That same year, he also assumed the positions of chairman of the Central Military Commission (the Party's top military post) and state president. But his real profile as China's paramount leader began only with Deng's death in 1997. Compared with Mao and Deng, Jiang was certainly less "paramount." Nonetheless, he became more "embedded" in the policy-making bureaucracies, holding almost all the top titles.

Tanks and soldiers of the People's Liberation Army guard a strategic avenue leading into Tiananmen Square, June 1989. On June 3 and 4, Chinese troops forcibly dispersed a demonstration in the square by pro-democracy students. Hundreds are believed to have been killed in the crackdown.

Jiang is said to be among the "third generation" of Chinese leaders. In style and substance, he differed from his predecessors in the first generation of Chinese leaders (Mao) and the second generation (Deng). In broad historical terms, Mao never trusted the bureaucracy and ended up destroying most of it. Deng rebuilt it but did not really need it to get things done. Jiang sought to dominate almost every policy-making area and, to a certain degree, became more constrained by the growing policy-making community.

Several trends in China's politics under Jiang can be discerned. One was a broadening and diffusing of the policy-deliberation and policy-making arenas. Perhaps more than any other top leader before him, Jiang tended to seek advice from specialists, experts, and bureaucrats in formulating policy. In an age of globalization and interdependence, individual leaders, no matter how paramount, need support from experts in highly technical areas.

In the early 1980s, reform leaders such as Zhao Ziyang and Hu Yaobang had set up several think tanks in both the State Council and the Secretariat to channel intellectual input into the process of policy making. The goal was to avoid major policy mistakes such as the Great Leap Forward and the Cultural Revolution. Public and internal debates by scholars and policy analysts greatly expanded during the 1990s under Jiang, and in the early years of the 21st century, privately funded policy research institutions, including those for foreign affairs, also started to emerge.

Jiang stepped down from his last official post, as chairman of the Central Military Commission, in September 2004, but by that time the "fourth generation" of Chinese leaders had already come onto the scene. Foremost among the fourth generation is Hu Jintao, who became China's paramount leader upon assuming the post of chairman of the Central Military Commission at Jiang's retirement. Hu had earlier gained the other top posts—general secretary of the CCP (October 2002) and state president (March 2003).

Jiang Zemin meets with President Bill Clinton in Washington, D.C., October 1997. Under Jiang, whose rise to power began in the aftermath of the Tiananmen crackdown, Deng's program of economic reforms continued.

The top leaders of the fourth generation, including Hu and Wen Jiabao, China's premier, emphasized the importance of a government that is more responsive to the needs of the Chinese people. Hu, in particular, discussed the need to stamp out Chinese Communist Party corruption. Yet he also clearly reaffirmed his determination that the CCP would remain supreme, calling this the perfect arrangement for China and ruling out a Western-style democratic system.

In 2008 Xi Jinping became vice president of China. Two years later, the former Communist Party secretary of Shanghai ascended to the vice chairmanship of the Central Military Commission. This put him in line to become China's paramount leader after Hu Jintao stepped down as general secretary of the CCP in late 2012 and as president of China in early 2013. Born in 1953, Xi is a self-described pragmatist.

Delegates to the National People's Congress in Beijing stand for the playing of the Chinese national anthem. In theory the NPC, China's parliament, is the "highest organ of state power," but it meets only once a year for about two weeks for its "working session."

4

Institutions and Structure of Government

The single most prominent difference between China's governmental system and those of Western-style democracies is the unique role played by the Chinese Communist Party. In Western democracies, positions in the legislative and executive branches of government are filled through elections in which candidates from two or more major political parties compete. In China, by contrast, the CCP holds a virtual monopoly of political power, and the various institutions of the state are essentially structured to carry out the policies of the Party. The primacy of the CCP (along with its ideology) is written into the Constitution of the People's Republic of China. The preamble to the 1982 constitution, as amended in

March 2004, contains the following: "Under the leadership of the Communist Party of China . . . the Chinese people of all nationalities will continue to adhere to the people's democratic dictatorship [and] follow the socialist road. . . ."

The Party's dominance of the state is ensured in two major ways. First, the CCP supervises all the major institutions of government (including the presidency or executive office, the legislature, and the military) with parallel institutions, from the national level down to local levels. Second, the ruling elites of almost all governmental and military institutions are members of the Party. Within these governmental and military institutions, Party members are organized through Party committees, branches, and groups. Before recent reforms, Party membership was a requirement for most government employment.

The dominance and pervasiveness of the Party does not necessarily mean that the Party does everything, however. Broadly, the Party and Party organizations focus on major issues at the level of governmental jurisdiction, while leaving specifics and daily routines to government officials.

Structure of the CCP

With more than 65 million members, the Chinese Communist Party is the world's largest political party. In structure it is basically pyramidal. At the bottom are the many local Party organizations from every part of the country; at the top are a few elite decision-making bodies based in Beijing.

About every five years, some 2,000 delegates drawn from local Party organizations across China convene for the CCP's National Party Congress, whose primary role is to select the Party's Central Committee. Consisting of 200 full members and 150 alternates, the Central Committee in turn selects—or, more accurately, approves—the 24 members of the Politburo, or Political Bureau.

(In actuality, it is the Politburo that controls the Central Committee.) To reach the Politburo, a person typically needs many years of distinguished service in the Party, in addition to a powerful patron, as advancement at the highest levels depends as much on personal relationships as qualifications. Politburo members are often drawn from the ranks of Party general secretaries for major provinces or municipalities.

From the full Politburo come the members of the Politburo Standing Committee, a small group (membership varies but was nine as of 2012) that includes the most powerful and influential leaders of the CCP. The Standing Committee holds the actual reins of power in China—deliberating on and approving virtually every major decision taken at the national level—but its inner workings are largely unknown. It is thought that members seek consensus

Members of the Politburo Standing Committee address the full Politburo during a 1998 Communist Party meeting. The Standing Committee, whose size can vary, always includes the most influential Party and government leaders.

but, failing that, abide by the judgment of the majority. Public dis-agreement among Politburo Standing Committee members is rare. Between them the handful of members of the Standing Committee also hold the top Party and state posts, such as general secretary of the CCP, state president and vice president, and premier and vice-premier.

Another important organ of the CCP is the Central Military Commission (CMC). Through this 11-member group, the Party exerts control over China's armed forces. Major decisions regarding the People's Liberation Army, including troop deployments and the appointment of high-level commanders, are approved by the com-mission. The CMC also supervises the activities of the People's Armed Police, a paramilitary body whose responsibilities include internal security. While the majority of the CMC's members are generals, the top posts are filled by CCP leaders, and holding the chairmanship of the CMC is an indication that a person is the Party's paramount leader.

The State Council

While the Communist Party supervises the other branches of the Chinese political system, daily governance falls into the hands of the State Council (also known as the Central People's Government). Composed of a varying number of ministries, commissions, and bureaus—such as the Ministry of Foreign Affairs, Ministry of National Defense, Ministry of Public Security, National Bureau of Corruption Prevention, Ministry of Justice, and State Commission of Ethnic Affairs—the State Council is roughly equivalent to the U.S. federal government bureaucracies. Among its most important func-tions are drafting and managing China's state budget and national economic plan. Although the heads of each ministry and commission sit in the full State Council, which meets once a month, only a few of these ministers enter the inner cabinet, the Standing Committee of the

State Council. The Standing Committee, which meets more frequently, includes China's premier, vice-premiers, state councilors, and the committee's secretary-general.

National People's Congress

In theory, the State Council is accountable to China's parliament, the National People's Congress (NPC). China's constitution refers to the NPC as "the highest organ of state power." Officially, it has the authority to amend the constitution; make laws; appoint, approve, or remove high government officials; and question bureaucrats. Yet until quite recently, the NPC was nothing more than a "rubber stamp," invariably giving its approval to decisions the Party had already made. While the last few years have seen signs of an increasingly more assertive NPC—through, for example, sharper criticism of government bureaucrats, more votes against governmental policies, and even the occasional rejection of a government appointee—the NPC falls considerably short of an independent legislature. A large part of the reason why may stem from the fact that CCP members constitute the majority of the body (and nearly all of the leadership).

The National People's Congress is made up of approximately 3,000 deputies. They are elected to five-year terms by provincial, regional, and municipal people's congresses, or by the armed forces, which conduct separate polls. (Only deputies to people's congresses at the township and county level are actually elected by popular vote; deputies to all other people's congresses, up to the NPC, are elected by the people's congresses at the next-lowest level.)

The full NPC convenes only once a year for about two weeks, in what is referred to as its "working session." The NPC's Standing Committee—consisting of about 150 members—meets more frequently and thus wields more influence. (It should be noted, however, that since the 1980s the NPC has had several

A screen shows the result of a vote by delegates to the Tenth National People's Congress. In recent years the legislature has been more willing to criticize government policies, but as of 2012 it had never voted against a government proposal or document.

permanent committees, which have increasingly functioned on a regular basis.)

The structure of lower-level people's congresses resembles that of the NPC. "Local people's congresses at different levels," the Chinese constitution says, "are local organs of state power. Local people's congresses at and above the county level establish standing committees." Local people's congresses are responsible for ensuring "the observance and implementation of the Constitution, the statutes and the administrative rules and regulations in their respective administrative areas."

The President

China's president serves as head of state. The office carries various powers and responsibilities in domestic and foreign affairs. In the domestic arena, these include promulgating laws; proclaiming martial law, general mobilization of armed forces, or a state of war; and nominating, appointing, or removing high officials such as the premier, vice-premier, state councilors, and ministers in the State Council. Among the president's duties and powers in foreign affairs are receiving foreign diplomatic representatives on behalf of the PRC, and ratifying or abrogating treaties and other important agreements with foreign countries. Officially, the president does not actually decide state affairs but merely exercises power in accordance with the decisions of the National People's Congress and its Standing Committee. A vice president assists the president.

According to China's constitution, to be eligible for the presidency a person must be at least 45 years old and be a citizen of the People's Republic of China with the right to vote and stand for election (these rights may be forfeited by criminals). In theory, the president (as well as the vice president) is elected by the National People's Congress. In fact, the full NPC merely ratifies the choice of the presidium (an executive committee of the NPC). Just one candidate for president

Hu Jintao became president of China in 2003. His position as top leader of the CCP and the government was fully consolidated in September 2004, when he succeeded Jiang Zemin as chairman of the Central Military Commission.

and one for vice president are put forward, and the NPC deputies can only vote up or down. At the Tenth National People's Congress in 2003, Hu Jintao became president after receiving 2,937 yes votes (against only 4 no votes and 4 abstentions, with 38 deputies not voting at all).

The president and vice president, like NPC deputies, serve a five-year term. They are limited to two consecutive terms.

The Premier

The head of government in the People's Republic of China is the premier. Nominated by the president and confirmed by the National People's Congress, the premier serves a five-year term. He, also, may serve no more than two consecutive terms.

As prescribed by China's constitution, the premier has overall responsibility for the State Council and directs its work, assisted by the vice-premiers and state councilors. He convenes and presides over plenary as well as executive meetings of the State Council.

Rule of Law and the Legal System

Except for a brief period during the Qin dynasty—whose guiding philosophy of Legalism specified that punishment should be meted out for violations of the law regardless of the transgressor's station in society—the concept of the rule of law was largely absent from traditional Chinese governance and political thinking. Essentially, rule of law is the principle that all members of society, including leaders, must obey the law, and that government authority must not be applied in an arbitrary manner, but rather consistently and only in accordance with written laws adopted through an established procedure. Under the Confucianism-based dynasties that followed the Qin, law had rather negative connotations. Rulers and officials were supposed to govern primarily through their ethical and moral example, rather than through the law. While legal codes did exist, their actual implementation tended to be highly relativistic and conditional. Justice frequently depended on the personal virtue (or lack thereof) of the county magistrates, who were the state's designated representatives in managing the localities on a daily basis. Nor were there any legal checks and balances to limit state authority. In the end, the traditional Confucianist system represented the rule of men rather than the rule of law.

The rule of law continued to be mostly absent during the first decades of the People's Republic of China. This was especially true during the Cultural Revolution (1966–1976), when Mao Zedong unleashed China's youth, organized into the Red Guards, to attack the entire bureaucracy. The country's governing systems—Party as well as state—were paralyzed: China's nominal lawmaking body, the NPC, ceased to function entirely, and much of China's law-enforcement apparatus (including police and courts) essentially shut down as well. Much of the nation was ruled by ad hoc "revolutionary committees." This was also a period when the nation was in the hands of the so-called people's power. There was widespread political persecution against almost all social groups except the "working class" (workers and peasants). Governmental officials, intellectuals (including teachers, artists, writers, and performers), and those with not-so-politically-correct backgrounds (landlords, capitalists, people with overseas connections) were natural targets for random political persecution. The rule of law did not exist even on paper.

After Mao's death and the end of the Cultural Revolution, Deng Xiaoping and other reform-minded leaders undertook a serious reexamination of China's political system and its deficiencies. One consensus they reached was that China must pursue the rule of law, not the rule of men. Legal systems needed to be created and developed at all levels, they believed, and over the years this process has gradually taken on a life of its own.

In 1978 the Chinese government began codifying criminal and civil procedures for the first time since the founding of the People's Republic of China in 1949. The criminal code became operational in January 1980. A basic civil code was in effect by 1987, allowing the handling of disputes regarding such matters as divorce, contracts, patents, property, inheritance, and, most recently, foreign investments and intellectual property rights. In civil cases, mediation, rather than formal trial, is encouraged, partly for cultural reasons (in China social harmony has traditionally been viewed as being more important than clearly defined right or wrong). Indeed, between 80 percent and 90 percent of civil disputes, and even some minor criminal cases, are settled by mediation.

China's legal system has a three-tiered court structure. The highest court is the national-level Supreme People's Court. Its responsibilities include trying cases that have the most serious national implications; interpreting the application of the law in judicial proceedings; supervising the administration of justice by lower-level courts; and hearing appeals of cases decided by lower courts. The judges of the Supreme People's Court are appointed by the National People's Congress and report to the NPC and its Standing Committee.

Below the Supreme People's Court are the local people's courts, a category that is subdivided into High People's Courts (which function at the level of province, autonomous region, or municipality with provincial status); Intermediate People's Courts (whose jurisdiction includes prefectures and districts in provinces and autonomous regions as well as certain cities and municipalities); and Primary People's Courts (at the level of county or other small division), which in turn may set up people's tribunals. Most civil and minor criminal cases are heard in the Primary People's Courts; the other courts review cases from the next-lowest level and hear more serious cases.

Special People's Courts comprise the third tier of courts in the Chinese legal structure. These include courts that hear military, maritime, and railway transportation cases.

The Chinese legal system also incorporates the institution of "people's procuratorates," which China's constitution defines as "state organs for legal supervision." In basic terms, the procuratorates have a dual function: first, to initiate and facilitate prosecution, including authorizing arrests and deciding whether cases should be brought to court; and second, to ensure that legal procedures are conducted in conformance with the law, which includes monitoring state investigative and security agencies and courts, as well as defending citizens' rights. During a trial, the procuratorate serves as both prosecuting attorney and public defender. In essence, the procuratorate is supposed to provide a system of checks and balances on the government agencies, particularly in cases brought by the police. As with the court system, there are various levels of procuratorates; the Supreme People's Procuratorate, the highest level, has supervisory authority for lower-level procuratorates.

Recent Developments

Since the beginning of China's reform period in the late 1970s, the rule of law has gradually expanded. Several recent developments are noteworthy. One is the trend for municipal and local governments and legislatures to enact their own laws for local needs, particularly in the areas of civil issues, investment, and individual liberties and rights. In Beijing, Shanghai, and several other large cities, for example, the court system in the late 1990s began granting suspects the right to remain silent, to have access to legal counsel, and to be treated as innocent until proven guilty. China's legal experts are also currently debating the long-accepted practice of imposing harsher punishment on suspects for "non-cooperation." Pressure tactics or torture for obtaining evidence are increasingly seen in China as violations of legality and human rights.

Nevertheless, China still has a long way to go to become a nation truly ruled by law. Many difficult issues, politically and culturally based, remain to be resolved in relations between the political and legal systems. Provincial and local authorities, as well as certain business interests, have been known to ignore court decisions with

New members of the Chinese Communist Party pledge their allegiance before the Party flag during a ceremony in Guangzhou. With more than 65 million members, the CCP is the world's largest political party.

impunity. At the national level, there is a need for more institution-alized, more transparent, and more predictable transfers of power, particularly as regards the top leadership of executive, Party, and legislative bodies. There are contradictions between China's fast-developing market economy and its largely authoritarian (albeit more liberalized) political system, and between a more democratic process at the lowest level of the political system (village and town-ship democratic elections) and the still largely opaque political process on top. On a very basic level, China needs more qualified lawyers. The current legal and legislative systems in China, howev-er, have come a long way from both the traditional Confucianist and orthodox Communist systems, and momentum is continuing to build for increased protection of the Chinese by legal codes and institutions.

U.S. Marines on patrol during the assault at Inchon, Korea, September 1950. The Korean War, a U.S. economic embargo, and American support for Jiang Jieshi's Nationalists in Taiwan virtually ensured that the Communist government of mainland China would align itself with the Soviet Union during the 1950s.

5

Foreign Relations: Integrating with the World

In the more than six decades since the founding of the People's Republic of China in 1949, Chinese foreign policy has undergone several significant shifts. Initially, in the face of a hostile United States, Mao Zedong aligned his country firmly with the Soviet Union. Later, a falling-out with the USSR created opportunities for a thawing of relations with the United States. Yet throughout Mao's tenure, China's foreign policy was largely isolationist. After Mao's death, Deng Xiaoping sought to open up China to the outside world, largely for economic reasons. His successors have continued on that path, engaging the world and hoping to create a peaceful international climate that will help further China's economic development.

Mao's Foreign Policy: Ideological and Isolationist

If the Cold War influenced Mao's decision to align his country with the Soviet Union in 1949, the Korean War cemented China in the Soviet bloc. The Korean War, which began in June 1950 when troops of North Korean leader Kim Il-Sung streamed across the 38th parallel into South Korea, had been approved in advance by Joseph Stalin. By the end of 1950, China entered the conflict in support of North Korea, and Chinese troops fought in direct combat with U.S. forces fighting in support of South Korea. The war dragged on until 1953. For the next 20 years, U.S.-China relations would remain frozen and precarious.

But Mao's ideological differences with the Soviet Union soon led to a deterioration of relations between Moscow and Beijing. By the late 1960s, tensions had escalated into a full-blown border conflict. From a "single-adversary" strategy in the 1950s (against the United States), Mao shifted to a "dual-adversary" position (against both the United States and the Soviet Union) the following decade. The major thrust of Chinese foreign policy was to address the perceived threat from these two opposing superpowers.

But the rivalry between the world's two largest Communist countries offered a unique opportunity for the United States, which considered the Soviet Union the most dangerous threat to its security. By establishing better relations with China, U.S. policy makers hoped, they could increase the pressure on the Soviet Union. In 1971 Henry Kissinger, then President Richard Nixon's national security adviser, traveled to Beijing for secret talks with China's leaders. The following February, Nixon himself went to Beijing, thus beginning the process of normalizing Sino-U.S. relations (which would finally occur in January 1979).

U.S. president Richard M. Nixon meets Mao Zedong in Beijing, 1972. Nixon's historic trip, which helped thaw relations between the United States and China, also changed the strategic equation during the Cold War—not only for Washington and Beijing but also for Moscow.

At the time of Nixon's historic trip, both the Mainland (People's Republic of China) and Taiwan (Republic of China) claimed to be the sole representative of the Chinese nation and people. Following some difficult negotiations, a joint statement (the Shanghai Communiqué) was issued by Chinese and U.S. leaders during Nixon's visit to China; it states that there is "but one China," and "Taiwan is a part of China." Despite tremendous changes in relations with China and Taiwan, the "one-China" policy remains the cornerstone of U.S.-China relations and has been the articulated policy for every U.S. president since Nixon. Still, reunification of Taiwan with the Mainland appears unlikely in the near term.

By the end of Mao's life, the overall balance sheet of his diplomacy was not very favorable. Perhaps the best that can be said is that

China's independence was preserved. Yet the cost of Mao's confrontational foreign policy was enormous, though his role was by no means the only factor involved. For years, China remained virtually isolated from both West and East. Strategically, it became, at one time or another, the adversary of the United States and the Soviet Union, the world's two superpowers. Territorially, Taiwan was beyond the reach of China's reunification efforts. Economically, the entire national economy remained on war-footing for decades. Politically, China's elite became so divided over a host of domestic and foreign policy issues that the entire Party/state bureaucracy was paralyzed for 10 years during the Cultural Revolution. Although President Nixon's historic trip in 1972 practically ended China's two-front confrontation against both superpowers in the early 1970s, China's engagement with the West remained quite limited.

Deng: Peace and Development

China's foreign policy during Deng's time underwent some major transformations in terms of its goals, scope, procedures, and style. Central to the changes that Deng brought to China's foreign policy was the effort to reduce the influence of ideology. Gone was Mao's aspiration to carve out for China a prominent place in the international Communist movement. Instead, Deng focused on more substantial, feasible, and certainly much more narrowly defined "national interests." Beginning in the early 1980s, China stopped ideological debates with other Communist parties; no longer did Beijing insist that China's own version of communism was the only acceptable model for the rest of the Communist world. Instead, Beijing recognized the independent role of other Communist parties in their specific national contexts. Meanwhile, China ceased providing material support for revolutionary movements abroad, as Mao had done.

Deng reversed Mao's policies by which China had offered economic aid to Third World nations, even at the expense of its own domestic development. As a result, China quickly went from being a net aid donor to a net aid recipient and began actively to compete for economic assistance.

For the first time in modern Chinese history, foreign policy under Deng assumed a cosmopolitan orientation. Deng insisted that China could not modernize itself without making use of the existing technology and skills of the world, including science and technology and management know-how developed in the West.

A major element of Deng's economic reform was to open China's economy to the world market. At the beginning of the reform, China set up four special economic zones (SEZs), which are free-trade or tax-free zones. In the 1980s a total of 14 coastal cities, including Shanghai and Guangzhou, opened up for foreign investment and

Evening falls over a busy street in downtown Shenzhen, a city in Guangdong Province that was designated a special economic zone (SEZ) in 1980. The creation of SEZs, which were open to foreign investment and experimentation with market forces, contributed to the unprecedented economic growth that China has enjoyed over the past three decades.

trade. By the 1990s almost every part of the country was competing for foreign investment. Deng's open-door policy reached a point of no return during the 1980s and did not change even with the Western sanctions following the 1989 Tiananmen crackdown. As a result, China's economy has enjoyed unprecedented growth. By the early years of the 21st century, China was one of the largest trading nations in the world; in 2002 it even surpassed the United States as the number one recipient of foreign direct investment. Today nearly half a million foreign firms have operations in China, fueling Chinese exports and employing tens of millions of Chinese workers.

In the early 1980s Deng's government faced the issue of how to resolve Hong Kong's status in a manner that would be acceptable to China as well as Britain. In 1898 the British had leased part of what became the Hong Kong crown colony from China for a term of 99 years. Ahead of the lease's expiration in 1997, Chinese and British officials began discussing Hong Kong's return to China. A major sticking point was Britain's unwillingness to allow Hong Kong residents' political and economic freedoms to be taken away. Deng, while remaining committed to regaining China's sovereignty over Hong Kong by 1997, was nevertheless flexible enough to negotiate a format acceptable to the British, dubbed "one country, two systems." Hong Kong would keep its free economy and autonomous political system as a "special administrative region" of the PRC. Margaret Thatcher, then Great Britain's prime minister, called Deng's compromise "an idea of genius" in 1984, upon the signing of the Anglo-Chinese Joint Declaration on Hong Kong.

Behind Deng's foreign policy changes was a fundamental rethinking of war and peace. Mao's perception had been that war was inevitable, and China should prepare against an early war, a big war, and a nuclear war. Deng saw the world differently. He started to modify Mao's imminent-war theory as early as 1975, in the latter stages of the Cultural Revolution, by arguing that a major war would not break out within five years. In the 1980s, Deng began to emphasize that a peaceful international environment for China was not only desirable, but also attainable. During the 1990s he oversaw the largest unilateral peacetime reduction of a military in the world, cutting the 4-million-strong People's Liberation Army by one-third.

Meanwhile, Deng also made China's vast military-industrial complex convert to civilian production. He insisted in 1978 that at least half of military-industrial capacity be devoted to civilian production; eventually this figure was increased to two-thirds. Between 1980 and 1995, the PRC spent some 14 billion Renminbi—the equivalent of about $1.7 billion—on the conversion to production of consumer goods.

The 1980s also witnessed a major shift in China's foreign policy focus, from global to regional issues. The Chinese foreign policy community questioned whether Mao's high-profile and survival-oriented diplomacy served China's interests. Meanwhile, Deng further argued that domestic affairs were the starting point for the country's international role. Without a stable and strong domestic front, China would not be able to expand its international influence.

If Chinese diplomacy took on a lower profile under Deng, the scope of China's foreign policy also broadened considerably. A whole spectrum of issues—ranging from the increasing volume of economic interactions with the outside world to China's participation in various international organizations—came to the fore. And with the increasingly complex and more specialized areas in foreign policy, particularly in foreign economic issues, came growing involvement of specialists and scholars in foreign policy deliberation. Throughout the 1980s, China's foreign policy process became more diffused, and therefore more time-consuming. Although Deng's influence in foreign policy was decisive, he nevertheless lacked (or may never have intended to acquire) the

An aerial view of Hong Kong's financial district, circa 1997. On July 1 of that year, China regained sovereignty of Hong Kong from Britain, under the framework of "one country, two systems." That arrangement, conceived of by Deng Xiaoping, was supposed to guarantee the former British colony a degree of autonomy and political and economic freedoms not allowed in other parts of China.

monopolizing power of Mao. Foreign policy was no longer the exclusive purview of a single, paramount leader, or even of a small group of top leaders.

New Century, New Leaders

As a guiding principle for foreign policy, Deng Xiaoping had cited an old Chinese saying: *Tao guang yang hui*, meaning "Hide brightness, nourish obscurity." In other words, China should lay the foundations of international influence unobtrusively, Deng believed. It should bide its time, taking pains not to alarm other world powers—particularly the United States—while quietly and steadily building its economic and military capabilities.

When Hu Jintao, Wen Jiabao, and the rest of China's fourth generation of leaders took the reins of power in the early years of the 21st century, they continued Deng's low-profile approach to foreign policy—at least initially. In a 2003 speech at Harvard University, Wen presented the idea of China's "peaceful rise." Among its key points were that China's economic development both required and would contribute to world peace; that China would always take a peaceful path to development; and that China would not bully its neighbors or seek regional or international dominance once it had attained a high level of development.

During the early years of Hu's tenure, China took a "good neighbor" stance. It pursued better relations with India, a nation with

China's premier Wen Jiabao addresses the United Nations, 2010. Under the direction of fourth-generation leaders like Wen and Hu Jintao, China has taken a more involved role in world affairs.

An American aircraft carrier, accompanied by other U.S. Navy vessels, operates in the South China Sea, 2010. That year, China claimed that the entire sea fell under its jurisdiction—a claim that was rejected by the United States and other nations. During the past decade, China has quietly been building a stronger navy that could allow the country to exert control over this important waterway. It has purchased several older aircraft carriers that had originally been built for the Soviet Union's navy in the late 1980s, and has updated them for military service.

which China has historically clashed. In 2004 China signed a trade agreement with 10 Southeast Asian countries. China took a leading role in efforts to peacefully resolve the international standoff over North Korea's nuclear-weapons program. Chinese diplomacy led to six-party talks involving North Korea, South Korea, China, the United States, Japan, and Russia. Although the six-party talks stalled, American officials expressed appreciation for China's constructive role. Taiwan 's status remained a volatile issue, but overall the narrative of China's peaceful rise seemed plausible.

However, as China solidified its status as a world economic powerhouse, Hu and the fourth-generation leaders appeared to scrap Deng's *Tao guang yang hui* guideline for foreign policy. China became increasingly assertive in international affairs. Perhaps the single most illustrative example of that assertiveness was China's claim, advanced in 2010, that all of the South China Sea constitutes Chinese territorial waters, and all of the natural resources in that body of water belong to China. The claim put China at odds with its neighbors Vietnam and the Philippines, along with other countries whose commercial-shipping interests require use of the South China Sea. American officials publicly rejected China's claim, sparking an angry exchange with the Chinese foreign minister.

Meanwhile, China has been building the kind of modern navy that would enable it to project power out into the Pacific Ocean, much as the United States does. In 2011, for example, China conducted sea trials for its first aircraft carrier.

Presidents Hu Jintao of China and Vladimir Putin of Russia review an honor guard in Beijing. The history of these two leaders' respective nations is a study in contrasts. In Russia communism collapsed under the weight of an inefficient economy and a bankrupt ideology, yet the transition to democracy and free-market capitalism has been extremely rocky. In China the CCP continues to cling to political power and cite communism as the basis of government, even as it embraces capitalism and permits a modicum of democracy.

6

Looking to the Future

The rise of China's fourth generation of leaders was anything but dramatic. Indeed, they simply emerged through extended service within the Party and governmental bureaucracies before coming to the national spotlight. In comparison, the earlier generations of Chinese leaders were products of crises: Mao during the Long March, Deng in the aftermath of the Cultural Revolution, and Jiang in the midst of the 1989 Tiananmen crackdown and leadership crisis.

Fourth Generation: "Homemade" and Humble

The fourth generation ruled as technocrats. They demonstrated little charisma. Nor, seemingly, did they have any desire to leave their mark as "great" leaders. Indeed, the era of Chinese strongmen appears to have ended with Deng's death in 1997. To a certain degree,

China under the third generation of leaders seemed to have done better without those movers and shakers of history.

Aside from charisma, or the lack of it, a key feature of China's fourth generation of top leaders was their "homemade" background. To a large extent, leaders from Mao and Deng's generations started their careers with some experience in the West. Jiang Zemin and his contemporaries represent the last generation of leaders educated either in the Soviet Union or during the Sino-Soviet honeymoon. Their departure from China's political scene marked the end of a nearly century-old "Russian complex" in China. The new Chinese elites could neither sing "Moscow Night" in Russian nor speak fluent English. Instead, their minds were shaped by the decades during which China reformed itself away from the Soviet model. In a sense, China under Hu's fourth generation became more Chinese.

Perhaps the most important common background for the fourth-generation leaders was their shared political and personal experiences of the Cultural Revolution (1966–1976). This national trauma produced the "lost," or uneducated, generation of Chinese youth, as well as perhaps the most open-minded, or the least dogmatic, leadership regarding domestic and foreign affairs. Because of this, the fourth generation leaders seemed less devoted to any "ism" and more willing to fix problems with greater technological and intellectual abilities. Last if not least, Hu's generation did not produce great thinkers or statesmen. But it also did not make huge mistakes, as did Mao's.

Hu's "New Deal": A Kinder and Gentler Generation?

Despite decades of steady economic growth, Hu's China became one of the most inegalitarian nations in the world. While many prospered from China's evolution to a more market-oriented economy, many others—particularly in rural areas and in China's less developed western regions—remained in abject poverty. Millions of impoverished rural villagers migrated to China's cities in search of factory or construction jobs, and once there many were exploited by unscrupulous employers. China's fourth-generation leaders sought to address these issues. They

During his decade as president of China, Hu Jintao oversaw continued economic growth as well as a greater role in world affairs. During his presidency China established strong trade ties with developing nations in Africa, Latin America, and Asia.

made several highly publicized trips to some of the poorest parts of China. Hu and Wen made it a priority to reduce the burden on China's farmers and to boost government spending, slash rural taxes, and increase job training in the disadvantaged countryside. In a symbolic gesture meant to emphasize the govern-

An elderly woman begs on a street in China. China's decades-long economic boom has brought prosperity to many but has also exacerbated inequality.

ment's determination to end the widespread practice of exploiting workers by withholding or delaying their wages, Premier Wen made several visits to companies to make sure that employees were being paid on time. Still, the mistreatment of workers remains pervasive.

Corruption, which Chinese officials have likened to a spreading cancer, is another major issue. Corruption appears to permeate the Communist Party and the government, producing much anger

White-gloved Chinese security guards block journalists from filming a man with a protest banner outside the Great Hall of the People in Beijing. While the fourth generation of Chinese leaders permitted greater media freedom, a level of official censorship has persisted.

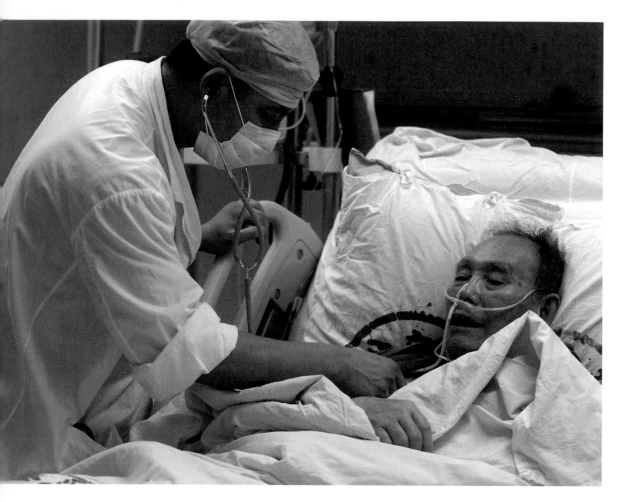

A nurse tends to a patient at the Guangdong Research Institute, where many victims of SARS were treated during the 2002–2003 crisis. The virus is believed to have originated in southern China's Guangdong Province in November 2002. Although some government officials initially tried to cover up the extent of the epidemic, the national government ultimately went public to educate people and contain the spread of the disease.

among the Chinese people. China's fourth-generation leaders prosecuted more and more public officials, some of whom were sentenced to death.

Hu and the fourth generation of leaders were cognizant of the need to burnish the CCP's image in order to maintain its legitimacy to rule. Hu stressed that the CCP should be modest, pragmatic, honest, and hardworking, and that it should really serve the people.

His stated agenda included promoting self-governance in rural areas, cutting bureaucracies at all levels, striking down corruption, and addressing social, economic, and legal deficiencies and injustices in China.

Hu even went so far as to unveil his own "three people principles" (power for, sympathy with, and benefit for the people). Jiang Zemin's theory of "three represents" (meaning that the CCP represents the most productive parts of Chinese society, China's advanced culture, and the overwhelming majority of the Chinese people) remained part of Hu's vocabulary. But Hu sought to portray a softer and gentler public policy that would contrast with Jiang's merit-based and business-friendly approach.

Democracy: An Idea Whose Time Hasn't Come

In June 2003, the Party theoretical journal *Qiushi* argued strongly that China should pursue democracy within the CCP, leading toward the eventual establishment of a democratic process at the national level. This inner-Party democracy, according to the article, would be achieved with five checks-and-balances mechanisms, including those inside the Party, by the people, by law, by other democratic parties, and by public opinion. All Party members, the article claimed, should be subject to the rule of law, and the National People's Congress should be the highest lawmaking body in China. In August 2003, *Xuexi Shibao* (Study Tribune), another authoritative weekly run by the Party School, specified that inner-Party democracy meant the separation of decision-making, policy execution, and policy monitoring powers within the CCP. During the 3rd Plenary Session of the 16th Party Congress in late 2003, Hu made an unprecedented move by reporting to the CCP's Central Committee on behalf of the Politburo, an interactive mechanism that had long been ignored by other paramount leaders. In February 2004, the CCP officially released its "Internal Monitoring Regulation."

Tens of thousands of Hong Kong residents march to protest the growing gap between the wealthy and the poor in China, July 1, 2011. The government allows residents of this semiautonomous city certain freedoms not available to other Chinese, including the right to hold public protests.

Many experts expect Xi Jinping to become China's next presdient and the foremost figure of the country's fifth generation of leaders. Xi is known for taking a hard line against corruption and for willingness to consider political and economic reforms.

It is true that Hu ruled more through consensus with other top CCP officials than had China's previous paramount leaders. And as the fifth generation of leaders took the reins of power beginning in late 2012, they continued this emphasis on collaboration within the Party's top echelons. Nevertheless, little progress toward democratization in China can be discerned. The CCP has shown no signs of permitting independent opposition political parties, a prerequisite for democracy according to the Western understanding of the term.

Fifth-Generation Challenges

China's fifth-generation leaders face a host of formidable challenges. Economic concerns are at the forefront. The explosive growth that China experienced from the 1990s on was fueled mostly by exports. But high levels of debt in the United States and much of the European Union may mean that China will be less able to sell its goods to these markets. Thus, maintaining economic growth in China may hinge on increasing domestic consumption.

China also faces a looming demographic problem. Because of the country's long-standing policy of permitting couples to have just one child, the average age of the Chinese population is increasing rapidly. By 2020, one in five Chinese will be over 60. Among other issues, this could lead to a labor shortage.

China's fifth-generation leaders will also have to prudently manage their country's growing role on the world stage. The bilateral relationship with the United States may prove especially prickly. American leaders have grown increasingly exasperated by what they regard as China's unfair trading practices.

If Chinese leaders will have to address U.S. concerns, American leaders will likewise have to accommodate China. China has indisputably moved into the ranks of the world's leading powers.

A cargo ship travels on the Yangtze River, a major waterway that is vital to China's economy. One of the challenges ahead for China's fifth-generation leaders will be to ease trade tensions with the United States and the European Union, the major recipients of its exports.

Chronology

1911   The Qing dynasty collapses; a republic is proclaimed by the Guomindang (GMD).

1916   Without a strong national government, China enters a period of warlordism and civil war that will last until 1927.

1919   In what will be called the May Fourth Movement, thousands of Chinese intellectuals protest the World War I peace conference in Versailles.

1921   The Chinese Communist Party (CCP) is founded.

1926   GMD leader Jiang Jieshi commands a combined GMD-CCP force on the Northern Expedition to wipe out Chinese warlords.

1927   After defeating the warlords, Jiang Jieshi establishes a GMD government in Nanjing in March; in April he turns against his Communist allies.

1931   Japan takes Manchuria, where it establishes the puppet state of Manchukuo.

1934–35   To escape GMD attempts to annihilate them, the Communists abandon their southern base areas and undertake an epic retreat, known as the Long March.

1937   Japan launches an all-out invasion of China.

1945   Japan's occupation of China ends with its surrender in World War II; civil war breaks out between the GMD and the CCP.

1949   The CCP wins China's civil war; Jiang and his followers flee to Taiwan; on October 1, Mao Zedong proclaims the founding of the People's Republic of China.

1950–53 The Korean War is fought.

1958–61 Mao's Great Leap Forward leads to economic and human disaster.

1966 The Cultural Revolution, a disastrous 10-year political campaign initiated by Mao, begins.

1972 U.S. president Richard Nixon visits China; the Shanghai Communiqué affirms that there is only one China and that Taiwan is a part of China.

1976 Mao dies, effectively ending the Cultural Revolution.

1978 Deng becomes China's paramount leader and begins a period of reforms.

1989 Deng orders the army to forcefully break up pro-democracy demonstrations in Tiananmen Square; Jiang Zemin becomes China's top leader in the aftermath of the crackdown.

1997 Deng dies; Britain transfers sovereignty over Hong Kong back to China.

2004 Jiang yields his remaining top post to Hu Jintao, thus completing the transfer of power to China's "fourth generation" of leaders.

2005 China invites James Soong, head of the Taiwan's People First Party, to tour the mainland, marking a change in strategy in the country's desire to reclaim Taiwan.

2010 China claims the entire South China Sea as its territorial waters. The United States publicly rejects that claim.

2012 China's "fifth generation" of leaders begins to take the reins of power.

Glossary

abrogate—to abolish or annul a law or treaty.

Cold War—a global political and ideological confrontation between the Soviet Union and the United States that lasted from 1947 to 1991.

Confucianism—a philosophical and ethical system, based on the teachings of Confucius (551–479 B.C.), that underpinned the Chinese traditional system and that, among other things, held that rulers should govern primarily by setting a just and moral example.

Great Leap Forward—a national campaign (1958–1961) by which Mao Zedong hoped to speed up China's economic development by, among other measures, abandoning the Soviet model of bureaucratic centralized control in favor of local grassroots initiatives; instead the campaign culminated in economic disaster and a famine that claimed as many as 30 million lives.

indemnity—a sum of money (for damages or as a penalty) paid by a losing country in a war to a victorious country.

legation—a diplomatic mission in a foreign country, led by a minister; or the official residence or office of such a minister in a foreign country.

Marxism—a political and economic theory, developed by Karl Marx (1818–1883), which asserts that reality has a material rather than ideal basis; that class struggle has been the primary dynamic of history; and that capitalism will inevitably be replaced by communism.

May Fourth Movement—an anti-West nationalist movement that spread across China in 1919 in reaction to the decision made by Western democracies during the World War I peace conference at Versailles to transfer China's Shandong Province from defeated Germany to Japan, rather than returning it to China.

National People's Congress—China's parliament.

plenary—of, or relating to, a session of a legislative or political body at which the entire membership is present.

procuratorate—a legal supervisory body in China that plays a role in facilitating prosecutions and safeguarding defendants' rights.

proletariat—the working class (especially urban factory workers under Marxist theory).

promulgate—to officially put a law into action; to make public the terms of a proposed law.

Further Reading

Bianco, Lucien. *Origins of the Chinese Revolution, 1915–1949*. (Stanford, Calif.: Stanford University Press, 1971.

Chang, Iris. *The Rape of Nanking: The Forgotten Holocaust of World War II*. New York: Penguin Books, 1997.

Cohen, Warren I. *East Asia at the Center*. New York: Columbia University Press, 2000.

Kissinger, Henry. *Henry Kissinger on China*. New York: Penguin, 2012.

Lieberthal, Kenneth. *Governing China: From Revolution Through Reform*. New York: W. W. Norton, 1995.

Menzies, Gavin. *1421: The Year China Discovered America*. New York: HarperCollins Publishers, 2002.

Schaller, Michael. *The United States and China, into the 21st Century*, 3rd ed. New York: Oxford University Press, 2002.

Shapiro, Sidney. *Jews in Old China: Studies by Chinese Scholars*. New York: Hippocrene Books, 1984.

Tyler, Patrick. *Six Presidents and China: A Great War, An Investigative History*. New York: A Century Foundation Book, 1999.

Wasserstrom, Jeffrey N. *China in the 21st Century: What Everyone Needs to Know*. New York: Oxford University Press, 2010.

Internet Resources

http://www.chinaculture.org/gb/en/node_2.htm

This site, run by the Chinese Ministry of Culture, offers broad access to up-to-date cultural news about China as well as information about China's history, politics, and economy.

http://csis.org/program/comparative-connections

Comparative Connections, an electronic quarterly journal that analyzes East Asian bilateral relations, including China's relations with the United States, Japan, Russia, Korea, and Southeast Asian states.

http://www.chinadaily.com.cn

Internet version of the leading English-language newspaper published in Beijing.

http://www.chinaview.cn

English web page for Xinhua, China's official wire service.

Index

agricultural producer cooperatives (APCs), 50–51, *52*
Anglo-Chinese Joint Declaration on Hong Kong, 84
Anti-Rightist Campaign of 1957, 52–53
Association of Southeast Asian Nations, 89

Bai Lian (White Lotus) Rebellion, 24
Bolshevik Revolution, 35–36, *37*, 46, 47
Boxer Rebellion, *29*, 31
bureaucracy, 16–17, 20–21
  See also political structure

Cao Gangchuan, 88–89
Central Committee, 66–67
  See also political structure
Central Military Commission (CMC), 68, *72*
  See also Chinese Communist Party (CCP)
Central People's Government. *See* State Council
Chen Duxiu, 35, 36
Chen Yun, *54*
Chinese Communist Party (CCP), 36, 45, *76*
  checks and balances, 96–97
  and corruption, 63, 93–95
  Cultural Revolution, 54–55, 57
  Great Leap Forward, 50–51
  and Japan, 39–43
  and the Nationalists (Guomindang), 36–40
  and Soviet-style communism, 46–50
  See also political structure
civil service examinations, 16–17
  See also Confucianism
Clinton, Bill, *63*
communism
  and Chinese intellectuals, 35–36
  cycles of, in China, 45–63
  Soviet-style, 34, 46–50
  See also Chinese Communist Party (CCP)

Confucianism, 15–18, 19, 27, 33, 73
  See also political structure
Confucius (Kong Zi), 15–16, 20
constitution (of the PRC), 65–66, 71, 95
  See also political structure
corruption, 63, 93–95
Cultural Revolution, 54–57, 73–74, 82, 91, 92–93
culture, traditional, 14–15
  and Confucianism, 15–18, 19, 21, 27
  and the tributary system, 21–22, 29
  and the West, 23–27
  See also political structure

decentralization, 41–42, 47
  See also Chinese Communist Party (CCP)
Deng Xiaoping, 54, 55, 57–61, 62, 79, 91, 92
  and foreign relations, 82–86
dynastic system, 14–15, 16, 22–24, 32
  and Legalism, 19–20
  See also culture, traditional

economy, 93
  Five-Year Plans, 47–49
  Great Leap Forward, 50–53, 57
  reform, 53–54, 58–59, 83–86
education, 16, 18
  See also culture, traditional

famine, 53
Five-Year Plans, 47–49
  See also economy
foreign relations
  under Deng Xiaoping, 82–86
  under Hu Jintao, 87–89
  traditional, 21–22, 24–26
  with the United States, 13–14, 79–82, 87
  before World War I, 29–31
"fourth generation" leaders, 62–63, 87–89, 91–101
  See also Chinese Communist Party (CCP)

Numbers in **bold italics** refer to captions.

Picture Credits

Page

Contributors

DR. YU BIN is an Associate Professor in the Political Science Department of Wittenberg University and Advisor/Senior Research Associate for the Shanghai Institute of American Studies. He earned his Ph.D. from Stanford University (1991) and M.A. from the Chinese Academy of Social Sciences (1982). He is also faculty associate of the Mershon Center at Ohio State University (1991–current); visiting fellow at the Center for Asia/Pacific Research Center of Stanford University (1998); visiting fellow at the East-West Center in Hawaii (1994–95); President of the Association of Chinese Scholars of Political Science & International Studies (1992–94); MacArthur Fellow at the Center for International Security & Arms Control of Stanford University (1985–89); and research fellow at the China Center of International Studies, State Council, Beijing (1982–85). Yu is the co-author and editor of several books, including most recently *Shunjian de Liliang: 9-11 Hou de Meiguo Yu Shijie* [Power of the moment: America and the world after 9-11] (Beijing: Xinhua Chubanshe, 2002) and *Mao's Generals Remember Korea* (The University Press of Kansas, 2001). He has published many articles in journals such as *World Politics, Strategic Review, Comparative Connections* [www.csis.org/pacfor/ccejournal.html#over], *Asian Survey, International Journal of Korean Studies, Harvard International Review,* and *Asian Thought and Society.* He also frequently contributes to many English and Chinese language media outlets.

JIANWEI WANG, a native of Shanghai, received his B.A. and M.A. in international politics from Fudan University in Shanghai and his Ph.D. in political science from the University of Michigan. He is now the Eugene Katz Letter and Science Distinguished Professor and chair of the Department of Political Science at the University of Wisconsin–Stevens Point. He is also a guest professor at Fudan University in Shanghai and Zhongshan University in Guangzhou.

Professor Wang's teaching and research interests focus on Chinese foreign policy, Sino-American relations, Sino-Japanese relations, East Asia security affairs, UN peacekeeping operations, and American foreign policy. He has published extensively in these areas. His most recent publications include *Power of the Moment: America and the World After 9/11* (Xinhua Press, 2002), which he coauthored, and *Limited Adversaries: Post-Cold War Sino-American Mutual Images* (Oxford University Press, 2000).

Wang is the recipient of numerous awards and fellowships, including grants from the MacArthur Foundation, Social Science Research Council, and Ford Foundation. He has also been a frequent commentator on U.S.-China relations, the Taiwan issue, and Chinese politics for major news outlets.